MW00563450

Planning and Implementing

RETREATS

Planning and Implementing

RETREATS

A Parish Handbook

Nicki Verploegen

WIPF & STOCK · Eugene, Oregon

Wipf and Stock Publishers
199 W 8th Ave, Suite 3
Eugene, OR 97401

Planning and Implementing Retreats
A Parish Handbook
By Verploegen, Nicki
Copyright©1989 by Verploegen, Nicki
ISBN 13: 978-1-60899-904-0
Publication date 8/2/2010
Previously published by Liguori Publications, 1989

Dedicated to
Beth Batzer Sterck and
Rev. Joseph Eugene Peoples,
loved ones who have believed in God,
in me, and in sustaining
friendship over many miles and
multitudes of years

Contents

Introduction

~

Retreats have kept me Catholic. I survived on them in my youth.

—L. R., DEVELOPMENT OFFICER

During deep silent meditation, things become clearer than any spoken word or any sight seen. Inner senses become open for the love of God to fill.

—B. B., BANKER

Within Roman Catholic Christianity, a resurgence of energy and interest in the spiritual life among the laity has occurred during the last fifty years. Even before the Second Vatican Council, lay Catholic Christians on a grass-roots level began to take ownership of their spiritual vitality, asking for resources and opportunities to deepen their relationship with God and to revitalize their participation in the Church. In the United States during the 1950s, retreat houses experienced a boom in the interest and willingness of laity to step away for retreat weeks and weekends. The hunger for more spiritual formation increased, and lay people began to claim their spiritual heritage to contemplative life and prayer.

Nearly half a century later, the hunger is just as intense. However, the structures and timing for retreats and spiritual formation have shifted. In an industrialized society of urban demands, lay people find themselves torn between family, work commitments, and parish involvement. The complexity of society has affected the family system, often leaving parents and siblings in considerable stress. Fragmentation and distress have resulted. Sports, school activities, and civic responsibilities vie for the precious spare time of families, and the laity feel the burden of these strains. They want more spiritual depth, but lack the freedom and flexibility in their demanding schedules to get away for long enough periods to attend to their spiritual growth. It is a rare delight for them to spend a full weekend on a retreat devoted to their relationship with God.

Current life realities invite pastoral workers to reflect on what can be done within parishes and other pastoral contexts to respond creatively to the hunger within people. There is a need for increased attentiveness to the spiritual formation of parishioners and those served in pastoral situations. Many parishioners will not have monetary resources or time for spiritual formation outside the parish or pastoral setting. How can people in pastoral service construct opportunities for spiritual formation within these limits? What types of experiences will grab the attention of busy parishioners and provide a balanced, grounded format for spiritual nourishment?

Retreats have helped shape people's spiritual lives for generations. Individuals have gone for days of recollection with diocesan groups, religious communities, and parochial social groups like the Knights of Columbus and the Women's Altar Society. But few resources have been made available to help parish workers plan, prepare, and implement spiritual formation events of a retreat nature. Although there are ample resources for planning prayer services and liturgies, there is a decided lack of literature to assist people in the art of retreat work. Most retreat planners learn how to give a retreat through trial and error. In consultation with several retreat houses about resources for graduate students preparing for ministry, it was revealed that no manual or guidelines exist to help in the process.

This book is an attempt to fill this need and respond to the spiritual hunger underlying it. *Planning and Implementing Retreats: A Parish Handbook* is a manual that provides practical, creative, and simple tools for pastoral agents who are involved in designing experiences to enhance people's spiritual lives. Retreat experiences can be rich experiences for people from adolescence through aging adulthood. This text supports the attempts of pastoral groups to construct creative retreat opportunities without having to start from scratch.

The format outlined in these pages systematically facilitates this possibility. It is helpful to anchor the practice of retreats within the larger context of Judeo-Christian tradition. We begin, therefore, with the scriptural and historical roots for retreat as a spiritual discipline, tracing biblical references to many souls who have retreated to a sacred space for communing with God.

We then outline five planning and design strategies for professionals and volunteers who want to create a well-organized and spiritually sensitive retreat experience. At the end of each of these five sections, a selection from a retreat sampler illustrates the strategy. Selections from a retreat sampler will include designs used for specific groups or ages that may have a special purpose in mind. Within the designs outlined, we will be attentive to the spiritual needs of different age groups, situations, and life projects of the specific populations for which we are designing the event. But each of the designs could be adapted and reformulated according the needs of other groups, tapping the creativity of planners. The sections will conclude with notes from the author on the implementation of the strategies.

Subsequent chapters deal with special areas of concern in creating parish retreats, including the use of metaphors in creating retreats, worship and liturgy, and evaluation as integral aspects of the planning process. Since it is also important that retreat directors maintain their own spiritual vitality and model healthy integration of the messages encountered within the retreat setting, a chapter on the self-care of the retreat director is included. A supplemental appendix briefly describes the historical growth of the Retreat Movement in the United States in the last century. A bibliography of resources is provided at the end to facilitate further preparation tools and study in the arena of retreat planning.

The planning and design strategies and the special areas of concern for planning retreats described within are suitable for group retreats offered in parishes, hospital ministries, campus ministries, and other pastoral sites where there is an interest in the spiritual formation of Christians. These strategies may be utilized when planning short retreats, days of recollection, evenings of reflection, or opportunities for reconciliation and healing. They can also be used for longer formats of a week's duration or more.

Well-planned and orchestrated formation events can revitalize and deepen the spiritual lives of people in parishes, hospitals, campuses, and pastoral settings, and invigorate the planners and leaders who serve them. The experience of an effective retreat with receptive retreatants can provide great refreshment for the planners, as well as those attending. The strategies outlined in this text can help planners nourish their own spiritual lives as they prepare for the blessed task of journeying with those in search of the living God.

CHAPTER ONE

Scriptural and Historical Roots of Retreat As a Spiritual Practice

~

Retreats, whether giving one or going on one, have meant a great deal to me. Basically, retreats, whether the "totally silent" ones or the more extroverted ones, fill a basic, urgent need in me to come apart. I "retreat" from the workaday world and its responsibilities, so that I may be able to hear more clearly that "still, small voice." As my destiny is to dwell in God's presence for eternity, it is good to start practicing it now! The happy consequence of taking time apart and being in God's presence is liberating and lifegiving, as well as renewing.

—C. E. F., LANDSCAPER AND FATHER OF FOUR

Retreat is a praxis, an application of the intention of our lives towards God. It is an investment in a relationship; the practice of going apart to consciously connect with God has an age-old history. When we look at the history of retreat as a spiritual practice we discover one fundamental reality: Retreat developed out of a need, a hunger. That hunger created a desire to move beyond what was known to something fuller. Whether it was a desire to know, to decide, to be guided or to be touched and carried into intimacy with the Divine, the impulse came out of souls reaching out to mystery. The hunger for intimacy ultimately leads to God. All intimacies originate and end in this primal desire for the Sacred.

We can return to our most treasured resource of Scripture to trace historically the practice of going off deliberately to a special place for an encounter with the Holy One. We begin with some instances from the Hebrew Scripture, our Old Testament, and proceed to some New Testament references.

The Hebrew Scriptures

There are few direct references to the practice of retreat in the Hebrew Scriptures, but there is the nuance of a similar process in the prophetic literature. Leaders, prophets, and kings within the tradition moved into solitude for wisdom and guidance for several reasons. Rich within these stories are vivid visual metaphors which tap the religious imagination.

Biblical figures were instructed by God when they went away to mountaintops, caves, and hidden places. Moses is a classic example; he depended on periods of sanctuary with Yahweh in order to be instructed on his leadership. He was leading a churlish group of people through a desert and needed constant guidance from Yahweh on how to proceed. "When the LORD descended upon Mount Sinai…the LORD summoned Moses to the top of the mountain, and Moses went up" (Ex 19:20). Once on the mountain, Moses took retreat. What happens there forms the basis for all Jewish and Christian spiritual formation processes. Moses is given the Decalogue, ten commandments through which this traveling group of believers can live in better relationship with each other and in faithful allegiance to Yahweh.

This is not a singular event for Moses and Yahweh. Moses is continually called away for longer periods of time, to see the glory of God in a multitude of ways. He passes six days and nights on the edge of the mountain. Then, he is covered by clouds. He emerges with stone tablets that concretize God's mandates for the pilgrim community. Then, "the LORD said to Moses, 'Come up to me on the mountain'…. Moses was on the mountain for forty days and forty nights" (Ex 24:12, 18).

Moses is not the only person with a colorful relationship with Yahweh. Within the prophetic tradition, most of us can recall the blazing figure of Elijah and his flight to Horeb (1 Kings 19:9–18), running to escape the wrath of Jezebel, whose prophets he slew. Elijah retreats, expecting his life to be taken. He takes refuge in a cave, begging God's aid. God surprises him. Instead of coming in a dazzling way with wind, fire, or earthquake, Yahweh comes to the cave in a tiny, whispering sound and Elijah hides his face in his cloak. Elijah is instructed on the anointing of the next king and the appointment of his successor, Elisha. Retreat for Elijah is one of discernment, listening, and obedience.

The New Testament

During the time of Jesus and in formation of the early Christian community, a broadening of "retreat" experience occurs. Jesus himself goes off to desert places, the Mount of Olives, and Mount Tabor to seek the face of God. The instruction he receives appears in seven forms.

1. *Jesus' identity as Son is reinforced.* Jesus' retreat to the desert after his baptism requires ascetical discipline, prayer, and vigil. In these practices he is built up in his call to intimacy with God. In each of the synoptic Gospels (Mt 4:1–11, Mk 1:12–13, Lk 4:1–13) Jesus' temptation in the desert is accompanied by fasting. Jesus' own understanding of himself in relation to God and his role in serving God with his life is deepened in this desert retreat.

2. *Jesus retreats to avoid being made king.* The approach to his messianic call must be carefully interpreted daily amidst many political realities. Jesus flees to the mountain alone to avoid being forced into secular service and leadership, which would be a betrayal of his vocation (see Jn 6:15).

3. *Jesus retreats to spend nights alone in solitude.* We are told that he "stayed out in the country" (Mk 1:45), spending

nights alone (see Jn 8:1–2). He goes to the Mount of Olives alone, for a purpose we can surmise was connected to grounding his own soul.

4. *Jesus takes the disciples away for recovery from the exhaustion and stimulation of ministry. It is also a time of preparation for miraculous events to come.* After the apostles were initially commissioned, John the Baptist was beheaded. When the apostles returned, Jesus invited them to a deserted place so they might "rest a while" (Mk 6:31). We can imagine the integration and processing that must have gone on around the fire there at night, as they absorbed the story of John's death and at the same time marveled at what they had just experienced in their ministry. Immediately following this event in Matthew 14:13, Jesus feeds five thousand, a miracle of staggering proportion. Not long after that, Jesus walks on water (see Mt 14:22–33). Each of these events was prefaced by time away.

5. *Jesus retreats for a time of consultation.* In a moment of epiphany, Jesus links up with leaders of the faith in the breathtaking story of the Transfiguration (see Mt 17:1–8). He retreats with three chosen followers who witness the mystical side of his spirituality. They are privy to a profound moment of encounter between God and Jesus, through Moses and Elijah. Is Jesus perhaps consulting with them on the next step in his ministry? That remains a mystery, but one wonders if wisdom was not somehow transmitted in this period of retreat.

6. *Jesus retreats, seeking strength in trial and acceptance of God's plan.* Perhaps the most poignant account of Jesus on retreat is the period right before his death known as the Agony in the Garden. On the Mount of Olives, all three synoptic Gospels tell us of Jesus' suffering (see Mt 26:36–46, Mk 14:32–42, Lk 22:39–46). A brief and intense "desert day" for Jesus, this event epitomizes the pathos of surrender and struggle to hold on to life.

7. *Finally, Jesus' instruction on prayer encourages stepping apart from others and entering into solitude.* "Whenever you pray, go into your room and shut the door and pray to your Father who is in secret" (Mt 6:6). This instruction is pertinent to both daily prayer and longer periods of prayer on retreat.

After Jesus' Resurrection and Ascension, the apostles continued the practice in modified ways. The entire experience of Pentecost was comparable to a weekend retreat of discernment. The disciples stepped apart into an upper room to discern and await the Holy Spirit (see Acts 2:1–4). Paul makes a dramatic turn later in the story, shedding his identity as an enemy of the apostles to that of disciple. He goes off to Arabia on an extended period of retreat to have his identity clarified (see Gal 1:17). In the desert he is prepared and discerns his new role as a Christian.

Early Christianity

Within the early Christian church, the practice of retreating took on other forms. In the Patristic Era, the Era of the Martyrs in the first and second century C.E., the celibate lifestyle was a new option that protected women from marrying into the cultural pagan system of the time. Instead, they chose to live a holy life set quietly apart. While this is not our classical notion of retreat, it does bear some familiar markings of the asceticism involved in a retreat. Later, in the Constantinian Era of the fourth and fifth centuries, Desert Fathers and Mothers fled the corrupt cities where they felt Christianity had lost its prophetic dimension. In going apart and retreating into a lifestyle of asceticism and prayer, they kept the radical call of Jesus alive. They escaped the mediocrity of city-Christianity and ran to the desert for a strenuous encounter with God. Once established in their cell, they periodically traveled distances to meet with a wise "abba" or "amma" and receive "a word" to contemplate in their solitude. They received spiritual guidance along with a challenge in these consultations with desert wisdom-figures.

Throughout the Middle Ages, monastic roots spread by the established practice of the Benedictine Rule. Monasteries provided safe havens for pilgrims and wayfarers. Later, in the fourteenth and fifteenth centuries, another lifestyle emerged that carried on the practice of retreat. The Anchoritic tradition, of which Julian of Norwich was one, produced cloistered women, dedicated to a life of prayer for the world.

In the sixteenth century, the Franciscan and Carmelite traditions began to speak of the art of "recollection," which now has come to be valued as a main focus in retreats, whether communal or individual. Francisco de Osuna, a Franciscan, first coined the term "recollection" in regard to the spiritual life and maturation. Carmelites Teresa of Ávila and John of the Cross referred to the inspiration of Osuna in their realization of depth.

But perhaps the most influential figure to bring the practice of retreats out of monasteries and into the public domain for contemporary Christians was Saint Ignatius of Loyola. The founder of the Society of Jesus in 1540, Saint Ignatius of Loyola formalized a systematic retreat experience based on spiritual exercises which he had undergone and reflected upon. He encouraged spiritual direction for the common person, introduced a decidedly scriptural dimension to retreat, and focused the experience on personal relationship and commitment to service in Christ. As a result, retreat became a practice appropriate for all devout men and women, religious and lay.

When all is said and done, what carries us into retreat is hunger for a God that transcends all our boundaries. It is a hunger that begs God for more. Retreat is a time when we break the habitual rhythm of our lives and step into the fire of God's longing for us and our longing for God. It is a time when we step to the edge and we find ourselves resonating with the yearning expressed in the following story from *Desert Wisdom*:

Abba Lot went to see Abba Joseph and said, "Abba, as much as I am able I practice a small rule, a little fasting, some prayer and meditation, and remain quiet, and as much as possible I keep my thoughts clean. What else should I do?" Then the old man stood up and stretched out his hands toward heaven, and his fingers became like ten torches of flame. And he said: "If you wish, you can become all flame."

CHAPTER TWO

Five Planning and Design Strategies for Creating Parish Retreats

Retreats! Much praying, planning, and preparation! It is worth all the work when young people transition from "I don't want to be here!" to "Can you believe God is real?"—stating this as if he or she is the first one to discover the reality and personalness of God. At these times, when young people catch the fire of the Spirit in their eyes and hearts, God is both incredible and life-giving.

—N. G., YOUTH MINISTER

I have made spiritual retreats periodically throughout my adult life. As a youth minister, I have helped present them. In a soul-searching for my place, I have attended them. Nearly every time, I come away having witnessed very obvious proof of the miraculous powers of the Holy Spirit, in both myself and other attendees.

—P. G., CANTOR AND ENGINEER

The effectiveness of retreats is highly influenced by the preparation done months before the retreatants ever arrive. Good planning and thorough organization facilitate a confidence and readiness in a retreat team. As we begin to look at creating parish retreats, it will be helpful to consider some basic preliminary steps to take.

Basic retreat planning requires that we address the "Who, What, When, Where, Why, and How" questions in our planning. Who will be our audience? What will be the general focus of our retreat? When is the best time to do this retreat and for how long? Why do we use a retreat format to achieve our ends? How can we best accomplish this? Presented within the first half of this manual are five strategies which systematically address the answers to these questions. Attention to all five of these initial strategies will provide a foundation that is spiritually life-giving to the retreat team and to those who come to them for their time away.

Planning involved in designing a retreat for a parish group or a pastoral need can be effectively guided by five strategies that begin with the letter "S":

- Spiritual Need
- Scriptural Grounding
- Schedule and Format
- Structural Design
- Setup and Ambiance

Each of these five "S" strategies helps to guide our focus in designing an event to stimulate the spiritual vitality of those whom we are serving. While they do not need to be addressed in a sequential manner, it is helpful to begin the planning and design phase with spiritual need and scriptural grounding. These two strategies form the foundation from which the rest of the organization can flow. They also decidedly address aspects of the retreat process that could be described as spiritually "formative" rather than merely functional. They tap the expertise of the planners in their knowledge of the group for whom they plan and demand biblical versatility and attentiveness from them.

The schedule and format and the structural design strategies are often composed simultaneously, one addressing the overall flow of the allotted time and the other providing the shape of the content for the retreat. They are heavily interdependent on one another as far as preparing a polished, integrated experience. Dialogue and communication will be essential in coordinating these.

Finally, the setup and ambiance strategy addresses the preparation of the environment which enhances the meaning retreatants can derive from the retreat. Artistic creativity can be very helpful in planning, as well as practical sensibility for what is feasible and attainable, given the limits of the location where the retreat will be hosted. This strategy allows the team to create space for a poignant and personal encounter with the Holy, using color, sound, nature, and setting.

These five planning and design strategies instruct retreat planners on the practical as well as the inspirational aspects of retreat. From this base, worship and liturgy can be planned to complement the input and structure that retreat planners offer. When an integrated experience is set in place, retreat planners can sit back and, respectfully and openly, await the movement of the Holy Spirit.

Strategy One:
Spiritual Need

> Retreat is a time and space where one seeks to have an intimate relationship with God. The aim of the retreat director is to prepare the groundwork for the retreatants to be free from the noise of familiar life and find the inner space so that God can be more visible and audible. In my experience the most lasting effect of retreat comes when the retreatants gradually notice that it is God, not the retreat director, who leads the retreatants into a new experience of wonder in communion with God-self.
>
> —H. H., SPIRITUAL DIRECTOR

The term "retreat" is used in a number of contexts in today's culture. Businesses speak of taking their executives away on "retreat" for the purpose of articulating their goals and objectives as a company, or to take their new recruits away to orient them to the policies and the work culture of the institution they are joining. Consultants are frequently hired to give employees a "retreat" to assess their effectiveness and determine new courses of action for increased productivity. These are not the retreats which we want to address in this book.

Rather, we return to biblical roots to recapture the notion of retreat as a part of the spiritual odyssey on which all people journey. Foundationally, retreat returns us to the original impulse out of which it emerged: We want to meet our God.

Our purpose here is to meet the spiritual hungers that people find erupting within their spiritual lives. We want to facilitate an encounter with the Holy which will nourish those attending by predisposing them to a new level of intimacy with their God, themselves, other people, and their world.

The first strategy for planning addresses the spiritual hunger that underlies an individual or group going on retreat. This hunger may not be something which has been previously articulated by the retreatants or by the retreat planners. With this strategy, retreat planners name the spiritual needs that may be lying dormant in them and in those who come to them. It brings the needs to consciousness so that God can meet them.

Hunger is all about desire. Desires can be holy experiences. It is through desire that God helps us discover what stirs our hearts most deeply. The desire we refer to here is not mere appetite. It is not what we merely want on a material level or necessarily prefer on the level of comfort. It is, rather, that deepest thirst within us that is rooted in God. It is the hunger for good and for fullness. It is the desire to be fully alive, using our gifts creatively for a greater purpose. Our desires are given to us by God to help us contribute our part in the ongoing transformation of world. In the process our own spiritual transformation occurs.

Desire, as it has been written about by many of the great spiritual writers such as Saint Ignatius of Loyola, is a positive experience which sustains our movement towards holiness and intimacy with God, while achieving the good that God intends for us. Desire can give us the extra thrust we need to keep going when our enthusiasm flags or when we become disgruntled. When we get in touch with it, our desire can empower us to persist in our pursuit of that which fires our core.

But desires can often be clouded over from lack of reflection, lack of permission, or lack of discipline. We may not have taken the time to ask, "What do I really want?" and "What does God really desire *in* me?" We may be unaccustomed to thinking that what we most deeply desire is linked to what God wants for us and through us.

It is essential for retreat planners to tap into this fundamental hunger of the human heart. The human heart wants "more." As human beings, we seek the transcendent. This alone will fill up that which is incomplete, limited, and disordered. All other substitutes are superficial and ultimately dissatisfying.

People come on retreat to have those human hungers addressed. They want to reconnect with the deepest desires of their hearts. Retreat is a time to be supported in that reconnection and given food for thought, assimilation, and nourishment. It is a time for restoring what is precious in life and claiming the spiritual need that pulls them back into relationship with the Divine.

Retreat planners need to be able to name these spiritual hungers, their own and others. What words or phrases describe the spiritual desires within us? When we think of "spiritual hungers," what words come to mind for us?

longing for God	understanding	refreshment
connecting	depth	strength
intimacy	union	wisdom
belonging	comfort	peace
reconciliation	bonding	joy

Other persons have named spiritual needs that they brought on retreat as follows:

direction	seeking God's will	to feel close to God
"being"	answers	clarity
discernment	healing	trust in God
reflection	integration	leisure
renewal	creativity	conversion
identity	hope	

As a retreat planner, it is helpful to be able to name some of the desires within us that motivate our spiritual lives. Take a moment now and answer the following questions:

- What do *you* desire in the depth of your heart?
- Can you name some of *your* spiritual hungers?

By getting in touch with the deepest desires of our hearts as planners, we can begin to name the underlying desires that may be a part of those who are coming on retreat. This will require us doing our homework. Who is our audience? We will have to gain some knowledge about the developmental needs of those for whom we are preparing this retreat. We will need to ascertain information and insight on their concerns in relationship to others (peers, parents, romances, authorities). We will need to have some idea of what they struggle to integrate in all of this, what their prayer styles might be like, and what is important to them in their spiritual life. In summary, planners must have some knowledge of the group, their issues, what may have shaped their image of God, and what might aid them in stretching further.

Based on this knowledge, we can reflect together on the following questions, keeping in mind the group for whom we are planning:

- What might they desire interiorly?
- What do they desire on an external level?

It is also helpful for us to name what we would hope the retreatants would receive in the retreat experience:

- Are there specific graces that we desire for the retreatants?
- Are there movements that we would like to see occur in the group?
- Are there special graces that we desire for ourselves as directors of the retreat, spiritual supports that we know we need?

In naming the spiritual desires that motivate our retreatants and ourselves as planners, we basically answer the most essential of questions:

- What is the spiritual need that merits the design and preparation of a retreat for this group which we are serving?

The answer to this question clarifies the necessity of planning a retreat. Without concretely naming these, it is difficult to justify the efforts in the planning. It can also prevent us from formulating a clear focus for the retreat design. With the spiritual needs basically stated, the specifics of the retreat, targeted for this particular group, can begin to emerge.

Spiritual Needs for Specific Populations and Contexts

The spiritual needs of those who step apart for a retreat may be influenced by the circumstances around which the request for a retreat surfaced. Some of these needs may be *age-related* or correlated to a *developmental issue* in the population we are serving. A retreat on aging and the spiritual challenge of growing in "wisdom and grace" may be appropriate and desirable for an elderly population in a nursing facility or parish context. The spirituality of aging is only recently being considered as a very real developmental issue that churches and their theologians must begin to address.

Some needs may arise out of *the context of sacramental preparation,* such as readying a group of youngsters for first Communion or adolescents and young adults for confirmation. Often a retreat is a part of the RCIA (Rite of Christian Initiation of Adults) catechetical and initiation process. In some dioceses, engaged couples prepare for matrimony with a retreat prior to their wedding.

Many needs are *situational,* coming out of a group's need to pause and reflect on a challenge in a circumstance and on the value they could derive from focusing their spiritual self within this reality. Within this, a parish staff may need to come together for retreat when a new member joins them. A subcommittee may need to step back and enter into a deliberate time of prayer to discern a new direction. A liturgy planning committee may find it beneficial to enter into a retreat setting as they establish their Advent themes for the special liturgies of that season.

Other special needs may arise out of events of *loss, grief, conflict, tragedy,* or *celebration.* There may be value in a parish retreat as the church approaches its centennial anniversary. When a conflict arises within a parish team, it may be helpful to retreat as a group to see the conflict through the reconciling eyes of faith and spirit. A parish loses a young student in an accident and a self-selected group of grievers asks for a retreat focused on tragedy, bereavement, and loss.

The first question planners must attend to when attempting to design a formative, effective, and timely retreat experience is: What is the spiritual focus of this retreat? In the classic sense a retreat is *always* about enhancing our sense of intimacy with God. It may also incorporate other intimacies of concern, for example, bonding with other people in a group, a sense of intimacy with who one foundationally is, or a sense of commitment to the planet and intimacy with creation. Intimacy with God, however, is the foundational intimacy that is the focus of the retreats we are planning.

Helpful Questions

With this in mind, clarification of the spiritual focus might be guided by the following questions:

- Why have a retreat? What are *the reasons* that a retreat is needed in this situation for this group? Is there a spiritual basis for it?
- What is the *underlying hunger in the group* that is assembling for this retreat? What are their needs? Is there a spiritual basis for these?
- What is the *underlying hunger in the team* that is planning the retreat? What gift would we hope to offer this group? Is there a spiritual basis to it?
- How could the *sense of intimacy with God be brought to light,* spoken of, and deepened in this retreat time?
- What *ambiance* would most suit this process of deepening in relationship with God?

These questions help retreat planners in three ways:

- They *ground* the spiritual foundation for the retreat and anchor the planners.
- They help *name* the various agendas of the planners, preventing the planners from projecting their own agendas without due consideration to their audience.
- They *frame* the goals and objectives for the retreat events and simplify the approach

This is the spiritual and philosophical base from which a structure can emerge. To make the experience truly "formative," one that will have an impact on shaping the lives of the parishioners, the deeper spiritual needs will need to be acknowledged and responded to in the retreat design.

Selections From a Retreat Sampler

To illustrate the definition of the spiritual needs of a parish group, the following selection from a retreat sampler is outlined.

Saint P's Liturgy Committee is responsible for the planning of all liturgical events within the parish. After several years of working as a group, new members were asked to join to relieve members who wanted to retire. For some members there was a need for reconciliation over difficulties from the prior year. A yearly retreat for the committee had been considered. Considering the busy schedules of many members, a Saturday-long format (9:00 A.M.–4:00 P.M.) at a retreat house was agreed upon with the finale being dinner out together at a local restaurant. A subcommittee of planners for this event emerged from within the larger committee.

The spiritual need was twofold:

- To ground the group in the Sacred in their role as liturgy planners

- To connect and bond the new committee members with the previous members in an experience of inclusion and welcome

The following *design* emerged to meet the needs:

An Autumn Day of Prayer

Focusing and Bonding Among the Liturgy Committee Members of Saint P's

- The entire day was liturgical as retreatants looked at the sacred text of their own lives, their story of liturgy and how it nourishes their awareness of God, the Sacred, the Mystery in life and in the world;
- it was a day of reconciliation and union for the committee;
- it was a day of uniting each member's gifts in service of the liturgical life of Saint P's parish.

Preparation for Departure: The group met at the parish rectory and carpooled to the retreat house so that bonding could begin to develop. After arriving and settling in, the members were given small stones for later use and introduced to the schedule of the day. The focus of the day was fourfold: sharing stories, reconciliation and union, community building, and prayer. The day became an extended liturgy through which stories were told and Scripture shared.

After the initial rites of the Mass, the Liturgy of the Word began with the reading:

> *Do you not know that you are God's temple and that God's Spirit dwells in you? If anyone destroys God's temple, God will destroy that person. For God's temple is holy, and you are that temple (1 Cor 3:16–17).*

The group then began a *storytelling process* of breaking open "the scripture of their lives," sharing the story of how liturgy had become important to them in selected events of their lives. An air of confidentiality and respect was requested, so that retreatants could feel free to share only that which they were comfortable disclosing in the group. A facilitator from the planning team modeled the sharing by giving an overview of her own attraction to the Eucharist, how it had "kept her Catholic" at times when the sense of community in her Protestant friends' churches was drawing her elsewhere. Something "beyond" her kept drawing her back to the Eucharist, and even when tragedies occurred later in her life, liturgy was a place of comfort, strength, and support for her. God was tangible for her there.

The group paused after each sharing, to absorb and reverently dwell with the sharing. After all persons had shared, a contemplative, silent break was taken.

The group then returned with the song, "Song of the Body of Christ" by David Haas (OCP Publications) as a *responsorial song*.

The Gospel was read: the parable of the Talents (see Matthew 25:14–30).

A *brief reflection* was offered by the pastor on the use of talents in building up the community and the challenge of focusing on the real treasure—God. The obstacle to this freedom often is found in hardheartedness which blocks a willingness to give freely. Each member was asked to be mindful of the "stones" within themselves that block the generosity of their hearts.

A *reconciliation and absolution ritual* followed in which each person came forward to drop their stones into a glass jar, while their hands were washed by another. The Liturgy of the Word concluded with *the rite of peace* while singing a reprise of "Song of the Body of Christ." Lunch followed.

The Liturgy of the Eucharist began with an invitation to quiet contemplation while instrumental music was played. Members took time away from each other in solitude and reflected on the gifts and talents they could bring to the Liturgy Committee. Each member was given a piece of a puzzle, one side of which was blank and the other side held a portion of Eucharistic Prayer III. On the blank side, they were asked to inscribe a gift that they wanted to give and a gift that they were hesitant to give. After thirty minutes of silence, the members returned to silently join their puzzle pieces. Gradually, the eucharistic prayer was assembled and then suspended as a mobile above the altar while it was read for the Liturgy of the Eucharist. Following a quiet exchange of Communion, spontaneous shared prayer closed the Communion meditation. A recording of Michael Card's song, "Immanuel" (from *The Life* CD), concluded the liturgy.

The retreat schedule for the day follows:

RETREAT HORARIUM

9:30   Arrival and settle in

10:00   Opening words of welcome
Focus of the day
Sharing our stories
Reconciliation & union
Community building
Prayer

10:15   Liturgy of the Word—"Song of the Body of Christ"
Opening of the liturgy
First Reading: 1 Corinthians 3:16–23
Storytelling
Pause before the Gospel
Gospel: Matthew 25:14–30
Reflection
Reconciliation
Reconciliation & absolutions ritual with rocks & water
Peace Rite—"Song of the Body of Christ" (reprise)

12:30   Lunch

1:30   Liturgy of the Eucharist—invitation to quiet

2:00	Puzzle-making
	Eucharistic Prayer III
	Communion
	Closing Prayer—shared & spontaneous
	Final Song—"Immanuel"
4:00	Dinner and departure

Notes From the Author

While this retreat format was used by a committee who planned eucharistic liturgies, it could be adapted for use with a pastoral team or staff, a youth group, or a parish health cabinet. The storytelling format is extremely versatile and engaging for participants, but the communal sharing time is balanced well with time for solitude in a daylong format.

The content of the storytelling portion can be determined by the specific needs and focus of the group, who are assembling. For example, a pastoral team or staff could tell the story of how leadership in the parish church became a work to which they wanted to give time. A youth group might tell the story of their "Original Fire" for God and how faith sustains them in adolescence. A parish health cabinet could be asked to speak on how they as individuals first linked up service to the needy with their faith expression and how they see their ministry as nurses, mental health providers, and physicians incarnating it.

In all three cases, the modeling by the facilitator will be crucial in setting the tone and massaging the memories of those who will share afterwards. The facilitator's style can help subsequent story-sharers by revealing aspects which might stimulate a resonance among the listeners. By finding common areas of concern for the parish group, the planners can incorporate an effective storytelling component, one that bonds a group and opens the door to greater communication and understanding. Knowing more about what moves other individuals on the committee "on a heart-level" can diminish the distance between people and diffuse conflicts in the future. That common reference point from the retreat can soften hearts that might be tempted to harden when differences of opinion occur later on. A storytelling which reveals some of the spiritual motivation and vulnerability in each person present is a wonderful way to link participants to one another in a camaraderie that can last beyond the retreat.

To assist retreat planners in naming the spiritual needs of the retreatants and the retreat team, a convenient series of questions follow.

Strategy One Questions: Spiritual Need

As a part of the team's preparation for a retreat, the following questions can be answered as individuals or as a group.

For retreat planners:

- What do you desire in the depth of your heart?
- Can you name some of your spiritual hungers?

Keeping in mind *the group for whom you are planning*:

- What do they desire interiorly?
- What do they desire on an external level?
- Name what we would hope the retreatants would receive in the retreat experience:
- Are there specific graces that we desire for the retreatants?
- Are there movements that we would like to see occur in the group?
- Are there special graces that we desire for ourselves as directors of the retreat, spiritual supports we know we need?

What is the spiritual need that merits the design and preparation of a retreat in the pastoral context in which we are serving?

Strategy Two:
Scriptural Grounding

After these eight days of dwelling with Jesus in Scripture,
I will never read the Bible again in the same way. All my
studies were helpful, but they never introduced me to the
living Christ like I have experienced in this retreat.

—J. Z., HIGH SCHOOL RELIGION TEACHER

The foundation of our faith is situated in our tradition. In Roman
Catholic Christianity, this is firmly ensconced in two loci: holy Scripture and Church Tradition. Holy Scripture is the body of literature
that was canonically accepted as authoritative and blessed in the late
second century, C.E. It is the written word that emerged from an oral
tradition of stories and reflection upon experience. Church Tradition
is also an oral tradition of life experience, which was accumulated
before, during, and after the Scripture was formalized. It is composed from many sources, including papal encyclicals, teachings of
the magisterium, theologians, schools of spirituality, the writings
and lives of the saints, and the mystical, contemplative tradition. It
also incorporates the stories of many other Christians who have reflected on their experience of faith and have recorded their insights.

When we speak of "grounding" our retreat designs, we are talk-
ing about stepping out onto this broad platform of historical wisdom and checking our wisdom and ideas against that gathered in
the Tradition. We may have notions of how to meet the spiritual
needs of those for whom we plan. Scriptural grounding allows us to
pause and ask, "What does our Tradition offer us in this area?" In
response to that question, we may find ourselves gravitating towards
specific books of the Bible or the great writings of saints and sages
who have contributed their insights to our focus and need.

This is a deliberately contemplative phase for retreat planners.
We may be tempted to rush through these first two strategies, but
we must slow down and go deeper in order to facilitate this process
for those for whom we plan. In this phase planners are required to

step into a reflective attitude and dwell with the saints of old and the wisdom of the ages. It is not as functional a step as other phases of the planning process can be.

Much of what we do in retreat direction is intuitively based; we use our own story as a reference and then imaginatively tease out what means could be used to assist others in a similar way. Organically, words of wisdom and associations from the Church Tradition can come up when we speak of real-life situations that we take to retreat. The planners' role is in part to highlight the universality of our experience in light of the larger Tradition and use that Tradition to support the spiritual process that the retreat affords. The retreatants then tap into a larger base of knowledge, insight, and depth to guide their reflective and contemplative encounter with God and each other.

We think for instance of grief and loss and, naturally, words from the Book of Psalms, Wisdom, and Lamentations come forth:

- Psalm 20: "The Lord answer you in the day of trouble…."
- Psalm 22: "My God, my God, why have you forsaken me…?"
- Wisdom 3: "…the souls of the righteous are in the hand of God, and no torment will ever touch them…."
- Lamentations 3: "I am one who has seen affliction…."

Words also emerge from Paul's letter to the Romans and the letters of John when encouragement is needed:

- Romans 8:38–39: "For I am convinced that neither death, nor life, neither angels, nor rulers, nor things present, nor things to come, nor powers…will be able to separate us from the love of God in Christ Jesus our Lord."
- 1 John 4:18: "There is no fear in love, but perfect love casts out fear."

Words of comfort also reverberate from Scripture:

- Psalm 18:28: "It is you who light my lamp; the LORD, my God, lights up my darkness."
- Habakkuk 2:3: "For there is still a vision for the appointed time; it speaks of the end, and does not lie. If it seems to tarry, wait for it; it will surely come, it will not delay."

How do we find those sources? How do we locate those places in Scripture that are pertinent to the retreats we organize? Most desirable, of course, is a personalized familiarity with the texts that has been fostered over years of attraction, spiritual discipline, and reflection. Our desire and integration of Scripture in our own lives is perhaps the most valuable, authoritative source we could possibly have. A life lived in close dialogue with God through the written word speaks volumes to those who come to us with their needs. We can speak from personal experience about which texts move us and could be of help to them. A passion can grow in us as we expose ourselves to the rich nuances of different passages and their meaning for our lives.

This is only hard won through years of repeated visitation, listening to the proclamation of the Word at liturgy, praying the Liturgy of the Hours, or taking Scripture to private prayer or to study. Giving ourselves the opportunity to pause and digest the challenges in various stories, poetry, and reminders from within the text can serve to deepen our ease with Scripture and enhance our personal devotion to our relationship with the writers and the Mystery within them. It behooves any retreat planner to make it a priority to delve into Scripture and internalize the content therein through repeated prayer and reading.

When planners gather to reflect on the wisdom that the Tradition offers them, scriptural associations and connections can surface within the group's prayer. These questions may be posed:

- What passages come to mind as we reflect on the needs of those for whom we plan this retreat?
- Do any images from the Gospels apply to our theme, for

example, parable illustrations, events from Jesus' life, agricultural references, and so forth?
- Do any references from other authors come to mind, for example, Thomas Merton, Julian of Norwich, Teresa of Ávila, Mother Teresa, and so forth?
- Which passages are most pertinent to this retreat?
- How can we use these passages in our design?

Quiet time spent dwelling on spiritual needs in a prayerful fashion can help the planners to recall texts that intuitively come up from within. It is helpful to have one planning session devoted to this "contemplative steeping," answering these questions. Done in a prayerful atmosphere, this session allows the planners to settle in with the Word and let the ideas and connections from Scripture surface in a quiet, supportive environment. Individuals contributing their associations can trigger each other's recall, and gradually a composite "word" from the Spirit can be heard. The combined communal memory and free association can be a vehicle for creativity and fresh inspiration. It can also be an affirmation for the planners of their own spiritual inspiration and intuition about the direction for the retreat, using references that may have been powerful for them. If a particular scriptural passage was significant for the planners, chances are that, with some modifications, it could be framed in a way that would be meaningful for others.

This reflective process can serve as a litmus test for the focus of the planners:

- Does our agenda for the retreat mesh with the scriptural grounding in the Church Tradition?
- Are there ample spiritual resources that validate and instruct us?
- How can we as the planners tease out the underlying meaning and biblical significance for the retreatants?

Scriptural grounding is a valuable step in the planning process in that it allows the planners contemplative time to dwell with the wisdom from the larger Tradition. So essential is this that in this book an entire chapter is devoted to the use of metaphors, many of which come from the biblical tradition. Scriptural metaphors can take on new depth and vibrancy when utilized in a retreat setting. When this phase of planning is taken up deliberately, fresh images can emerge. The "packaged" standardized notions that people have from years of Sunday homilies can burst open and casual images from the Bible come alive with new associations for integration by the retreatants. Dwelling with these images from the Bible can infuse subsequent encounters with the Word with new meaning and power after the retreat. Planners will do well to refer to the chapter, "The Use of Metaphors in Creating Retreats" (p. 65), for input on other creative applications.

For those unfamiliar with the location of specific passages, planners can turn to concordances or resource books which list scriptural passages by theme or phrase. From these they can expand their awareness and tailor it to the needs of the retreat. Scriptural grounding allows the planning team to dwell with the text, letting it expand within them, and from that broader base creatively apply the text in the next phases of planning.

Selections From a Retreat Sampler

Our Lady of C's choir hosts a daylong retreat each year to prepare new music for the next liturgical cycle. In addition to practicing new music, *the retreat's purpose* is to allow the choir time to pray together and bond as a group. This year the choir director asks that the retreat begin with an extended Morning Prayer that ties in Scripture. He is also interested in possibly introducing the choir to liturgical movement as a valuable tool for worship. The following Morning Prayer is based on the Exodus Event (see Ex 1:8–32:14). It weaves in recorded music, chants, silence, readings, and movement.

Our Journey From Slavery
Through Liberation to New Fullness

Prepare the room with soft light, and circle chairs around a "center-spot" (see p. 57) of candles, bread bits, a small bowl of water, and cloth. Soft instrumental music can be playing as the group assembles. Leave room between the chairs so that limited movement can be done. Allow plenty of quiet time between the sections of scriptural text so that the group can integrate the words with their reality, as a choir ensemble on a journey—one with many old and new songs to sing. Either select eight readers for the text or let people read in sequence from around the circle.

Opening Chant:
>Taizé's "Confitemini de Domino"—"Come and Fill our Hearts" (GIA Publications)

Reader 1: The people were in a faraway land. Their ancestors who brought them there had all died. But they were fruitful and prolific. They became so numerous and strong that the land was filled with them.... So taskmasters were set over them to oppress them with forced labor..., reducing them to cruel slavery and making life bitter.... How could they sing their songs of praise in a foreign land? As their cry for release went up to God, God heard their groaning and was mindful of the covenant with their parents. God saw the people and knew.... (*Pause in silence.*)

Recorded Song:
>"On the Willows," *Godspell* recording

≈

Reader 1: Meanwhile, faraway, Moses was tending his flock... leading the flock across the desert. He came to the mountain of God.... There an angel of the Lord appeared to him in fire, flaming out of a bush. As Moses looked on, he was surprised to see that the bush, though on fire, was not consumed.... God called out:

Reader 2: Moses, Moses!

Reader 3: Here I am!

Reader 2: Remove the sandals from your feet for the place where you stand is holy ground. I have witnessed the affliction of my people in Egypt and have heard their cry...so I know well what they are suffering. They cannot sing. They cannot dance. Therefore, I have come down to rescue them and to lead them out of that land.

Reader 3: Who am I, Lord, that I should go to Pharaoh?

Reader 2: I will be with you. This is what you shall tell them: "I AM has sent me to you." Let my song be your words.

Reader 1: And Moses started back to Egypt. (*Pause in silence.*)

Responsorial Chant:
Taize's "Ubi Caritas" chant (GIA)

∾

Reader 1: Moses went with Aaron to Pharaoh and said:

Reader 3: Thus says the Lord, the God of Israel: "Let my people go...."

Reader 1: And Pharaoh said:

Reader 4: I do not know the Lord.... I will not let Israel go.

Reader 1: And God made Pharaoh's heart hard to use him to display God's greatness. Ten plagues God sent until, finally, the angel of death took the Egyptian firstborn ones' lives. Pharaoh relented and the Israelites departed Egypt. They were guided by a cloud in the day and a column of fire at night. But Pharaoh pursued them to edge of the sea.

Reader 1: So the people complained:

Reader 5: Were there no burial places in Egypt that we had to be brought out here to die in the desert?

Reader 1: Then the Lord said to Moses:

Reader 2: Why are you crying out to me? Tell the Israelites to go forward…they will pass through the sea on dry land. But Pharaoh shall not be allowed to pass.

Reader 1: So the one who pursued was swallowed by the great waters. The Lord saved Israel on that day from the power of their oppressors. They feared God and believed God…for awhile…. (*Pause.*)

Silent Reflection Period

≈

Reader 1: They came to the desert of Sin and they grumbled against Moses and cried:

Reader 5: Would that we had died in Egypt for we had bread there.

Reader 1: And God gave them bread from heaven each night and quail each morning. From here, the community journeyed by stages as the Lord directed them. Then, there was no water and they complained bitterly. And God spoke to Moses:

Reader 2: If you really listen to the voice of God and do what is right in God's eyes; if you heed God's commandments and keep all the precepts, I will not afflict you with any problems…I, the Lord, am your healer.

Reader 1: And God gave them water. Finally, they arrived at the mountain. Then the Lord delivered commandments.

Reader 2: You have seen for yourselves how I bore you up on eagle's wings and brought you here myself…. If you hearken to my voice and keep my covenant, you shall be my special people.

Reader 1: For a while, the people trembled.

Reader 5: We will do everything that the Lord has told us.

Reader 1: But when Moses delayed and left them alone for forty days, they built an idol and celebrated. And when Moses saw their infidelity, their return to unfaithful ways, he broke the tablets of the Law in rage. How could they truly enter the Promised Land if they could not live with this covenant, a relationship of reverence with God and each other? (*Pause.*)

Silence

Response: (*sung or spoken*) Today, if you hear his voice, if you hear his voice, then, please do not harden your hearts. (*Repeat several times.*)

Reader 6: Again and again, the Mystery reveals itself to us.
Again and again, our response suffers.
At times we yearn for the familiar that we left behind.
At times we hunger for new food, that will quench our weary hearts.
We want to sing our old songs.

Reader 7: And sometimes, we find substitute gods to honor in the absence of True Presence.
Our void seems too deep to let the Void of Mystery reso nate in the emptiness;
our word and our song feel silenced by the fear and vul nerability that no other Word will respond.
But the Word waits for our "yes,"
And dies to reach again.
A New Song can be sung.

Reader 8: "Where is the Promised Land?" we ask.

Are we ever "home"?

Is it a place to be arrived at or a dance to be learned?

Is it a static heaven or a constant swirl of movement that says, "I have learned how to say 'yes'"?

I have entered the dance and engaged with God in a relationship of dynamic intimacy.

I love into an ever-deepening constancy with that "Be-Loved One."

Maybe the lines of Exodus are circles of relationship instead of lines across deserts.

The sands that shift under our feet prepare us for the flexibility of light-footed reliability

On the One with whom we dance.

With God as our faithful partner, we can sing the New Song.

We can rise in the dance and sing out our "yes."

Closing Song and Movement:

"Dance in the Darkness" by Carey Landry (OCP)

An individual dancer can begin moving with this song, dancing the verses while they are sung by a soloist and inviting the group to sing the refrain when they get a sense of it. Begin with a very slow rhythm, singing almost in a whisper. As the choir gains familiarity, the pace and the volume can grow. Finger cymbals can also be used to highlight the refrain. If a simple gesture can be taught to the group during the refrain, all could join in the movement by the closing refrain.

Notes From the Author

This retreat was designed for a parish choir, which was incorporating prayer, song, and silence into their experience. It is a strong example of how Scripture can be used to illustrate human experience pertinent to any generation. Recorded music is used as well as sung pieces. Liturgical movement is proposed as a means of stretching the participants to another level of expression and prayer. This design could take thirty minutes to an hour, depending on the duration of the pauses and the pace which the readings are read. It would be helpful if the readers were prepared to read their texts with expression, but not in a rushed way. Ample time between the sections allows for integration and digestion of the words. The slower pace makes this simple Morning Prayer a retreat-like experience.

This same method could be done with other selections. Sections of the Passion of Jesus Christ could be amplified in this way for an RCIA group, in preparation for the sacraments at the Easter Vigil. Vignettes from Jesus' life could also be spliced between readers and done with expressivity. If it was appropriate, group discussion on the reading could follow the prayer event. Adapting the format to different groups, liturgical seasons, and time frames, planners can maximize the impact that a text can have on a group.

For the convenience of planners, a compilation of the questions outlined within this text for planning the scriptural grounding of retreats follows.

Strategy Two Questions: Scriptural Grounding

As part of the team's preparation for a retreat, the following questions can be used as a group.

- What scriptural passages come to mind as we reflect on the needs of those for whom we plan this retreat?
- Do any images from the Gospels apply to our theme, for example, parable illustrations, events from Jesus' life, agricultural references?
- Do any references from other spiritual writers from Catholic/Christian Tradition come to mind, for example, Thomas Merton, Julian of Norwich, Teresa of Ávila, Mother Teresa, and so forth?
- Which scriptural passages or writings from Church Tradition are most pertinent to this retreat?

- Does our agenda for this retreat mesh with the scriptural grounding in the Church Tradition? Are there ample spiritual resources that validate and instruct us?

How can we as the planners tease out the underlying meaning and biblical significance for the retreatants?

Strategy Three:
Schedule and Format

A weaver, an author, a yoga-practicing woman of deep faith, a teacher of forgiveness—this woman gave us plenty of time to reflect on her teachings in a smaller group.... I found that when we were alone to reflect, or pray, that I would seek out nature, the outside...that is where I feel closest to God.

—E. B. S., VOCATIONAL REHABILITATION COUNSELOR

The overall schedule of a retreat houses the formative and informative material that the facilitators offer. The content of individual input sessions can be inspirational and formative for the retreatant, but unless the design of the retreat is situated within a larger rhythm that fosters reflectivity and prayer, the retreat will not help the participant do what it promises it will. The schedule and format of the retreat must provide a conducive rhythm that supports the intention of helping people meet their God.

With this in mind, the schedule and format strategy looks at *the horarium* or *overall plan* of the time allotted for the retreat. The Schedule and Format stage formalizes the order of the retreat, including group sessions, meals, recreation, and worship. The following issues influence the scheduling of a retreat:

- The logistics of *the facility or location* of the retreat
- The *number* of participants and staff in attendance
- The *age and needs* of the retreatants

Location, Location, Location

Location can be a key factor in the initial scheduling of a retreat. The time of a retreat is determined in part by the limits and needs of those whom the retreat is meant to serve, as well as the availability of staff and sites. Within those limitations, dates and times are fleshed out and the length of the retreat is decided. The availability of sites is clarified and confirmed. Financial factors are kept in mind when securing a site for an overnight or weekend event versus a daylong experience.

We as planners should prepare well in advance for retreat events held in locations outside our own jurisdiction. If there is a benefit to hosting the retreat in a site away from our parish, hospital, or pastoral setting, we should *contact facilities immediately* with possible dates, keeping in mind the specific population that we are planning for and the flexibility of the facilities we are considering. Accessibility to those facilities may be a concern for some of our retreatants and transportation arrangements may need to be made.

Special needs and requests should be outlined as soon as possible so that accommodations by the retreat house can be realistically discussed. The limits of a facility may need to be taken into account when finalizing the daily schedule. For example,

- If more than one group is utilizing the retreat house, when would the chapel be available for communal worship?
- Are there fixed times for meals?
- Is there a policy in the retreat house with regard to silence?
- Must groups confine themselves to certain areas of the retreat complex?

Once a site is determined, the specific planning begins. In our previous chapters, we have been examining the formative and spiritual aspects for planners, but equally important is the practical planning of meals, prayer services, and so forth. The horarium of each day is structured so as to incarnate *a balance between times for prayer, relaxation, quiet, recreation, and nourishment.*

Numbers

Numbers of staff who assist in implementing a retreat are often as important as the retreatants who attend. It is advisable for retreat planners to assemble a team who can work together during the re-treat. This prevents an undue burden from falling on the shoulders of a single director and allows for greater shared responsibility. Small groups obviously require less organization and structure.

Most adult groups will take more readily to an open schedule for prayer and reflection than teen groups, therefore requiring less staffing. Youth groups usually require a larger number of adult staff persons, especially for an overnight event. The larger the numbers of participants, the more "chaperones" will be needed. A ratio of no less than one adult per eight students is suggested.

Obviously, *meals* become a consideration with a retreat planned in a daylong or overnight format. A facility that provides meals sim-plifies the planning significantly, especially for larger numbers, but it will increase the costs. Behind-the-scenes volunteer kitchen crews also can contribute to the overall effectiveness of a retreat. If volun-teers are tuned in to the thematic approach of the retreat, they can often enhance the work of the facilitators with special touches in the dining room, providing meals and an ambiance that further embel-lish the retreat focus.

Availability of conference and quiet rooms for larger groups may limit which facilities are suitable for retreats. Scheduling may be gov-erned in part by the flow of traffic in the dining halls and the wor-ship spaces. Planners need to get a "guess-timate" of the numbers as soon as possible and use that information in the finalization of their daily schedule.

When scheduling, remember these helpful hints:

- In adult retreats, don't overplan or congest the schedule.
- In youth retreats, leave time for socializing and recreation with some structure provided for each.
- Don't be afraid of quiet time, but make sure the partici-pants know it is intended for that.
- Include "lingering time" at the end of worship and prayer services so that retreatants don't feel rushed into the next activity.

Age and Needs of the Retreatants

In addition to the limits of the location and the numbers attending, the age of the retreatants and the focus of the retreat must be taken into account when scheduling is done. The structure of the day or weekend is geared around the style of the retreat that is appropriate for each group.

Elderly retreatants will need more breaks, time for visits to the rest room and ample time for movement from one area to another for meals, and so forth. Their needs regarding impaired hearing and seeing will also need to be taken into account when making arrangements.

Youth retreats require more activity and group time. Shorter spans for quiet time and longer periods for dialogue and teasing out of ideas are helpful. Since connecting with peers is an essential aspect of teenage development, youth retreats blend in more time for meaningful conversation and group prayer. Breaks can be shorter or woven into reflection time.

Middle-aged adults, on the other hand, have different interests when they attend a retreat. Scheduling must take into account these concerns. Most retreats of a more contemplative nature for a mature group keep activity and conversation to a minimum. In these retreats input is often done at the beginning of the day to orient the group thematically or, in the case of an overnight, in the evening to allow individuals to sleep on the themes and awake with them in mind. Built into the schedule is time for worship and reflection. Daylong group retreats for adults allow for activity, input, quiet reflection, private prayer, and communal worship.

With adult retreatants, a simpler schedule often facilitates greater satisfaction than a congested schedule. If quiet time is built in to the schedule, it is important that there be space for private prayer. The outdoors can be suitable if the location is rural or pastoral. Private rooms are very helpful but not mandatory. People should be able to find a quiet space that allows them privacy. Chapels, prayer rooms, or oratories also serve this purpose.

In securing the actual schedule for the different components of the retreat, dialogue on the focus of the Structural Design will inform us as planners. We know that our overall schedule will need to reserve time for recreation, meals, quiet, worship, and socializing. How these will be balanced with the content of the Structured input sessions is a key question for us to resolve.

The schedule of the overall retreat can be flexible enough to take into account changes that organically come up from within the process. However, it is necessary to be respectful of the structure that the schedule is trying to provide. Kitchen personnel, musicians, and chapel teams should not be expected to accommodate the schedule changes too frequently. A schedule should provide some stability and common ground for all those working the retreat and attending it, and it should not be altered too casually.

Selections From a Retreat Sampler

To illustrate and compare the differences in retreat schedule and format for youth and adult retreats, two different samples have been provided. Each of these could be modified for longer events as well as abbreviated for shorter forms.

A daylong youth retreat schedule could look like this:

A YOUTH RETREAT SCHEDULE FOR ONE-DAY RETREAT

9:00 Gather and settle in

9:15 Welcome and introductions of staff

9:30 Icebreaker games (*This should include introductions of participants using humor and limited sharing.*)

10:00 Session #1

Activity (*Game or role-play that provokes student reflection*)

Feedback *(Discussion in small groups or dyads for reactions to activity)*

Input *(Building on the game or role-play, tease out the formative messages)*

11:15   Quiet-time break *(Provide some structure for the reflection time that ties into the theme and meaning of the retreat, for example, find a symbol of who you are before God right now.)*

11:45   Midday prayer *(Create a brief ritual that incorporates the symbol.)*

12:15   Lunch and break

1:15   Session #2 *(If structured recreation is available, it could be scheduled at this time and Session #2 pushed to a later period. After lunch/early afternoon can be a difficult time for anyone to stay awake, so be sensitive to that reality in your planning and your expectations.)*

Activity

Reflection and response time

Input

2:45   Break

3:00   Opening of eucharistic or noneucharistic liturgy with the proclamation of the Word

3:15   Scriptural reflection *(Tease out the Word through homily, creative adaptation, or shared responses among those present.)*

3:45   Continuation of the liturgy

4:30   Preparation for dinner *(Organize the teens to prepare their own dinner in teams.)*

6:00   Dinner and cleanup

7:00   Evening prayer and songfest

9:00   Closing *(Prepare a final send-off blessing in which the staff and leadership pray or sing over the retreatants.)*

A general horarium structure for an adult retreat could be as outlined in the following schedule:

AN ADULT HORARIUM FOR ONE-DAY RETREAT

9:00   Arrival and settle in

9:15   Welcome and morning prayer

9:45   Opening session: theme and input

10:30   Quiet time: reflection and private prayer

11:45   Noonday prayer

12:00   Lunch *(Planners should decide if this is to be silent or conversational.)*

2:00   Afternoon session: theme deepening with Scripture

3:00   Group sharing

3:45   Break

4:00   Communal worship or eucharistic liturgy

5:00   Dinner and closing

If the retreat can extend into the evening, an additional evening session could be added. If a group would benefit more from periods of private prayer, group sharing could be reserved to the evening period and a second quiet period could follow the afternoon session.

Notes From the Author

The longer the retreat, the less intense the schedule needs to be. More time can be allowed for down time, rest, and integration. Adolescents tend to need more structure with shorter spans of input. Young adults often want more social time. The special developmental issues of the age group you are planning for are key factors in scheduling.

I recall a parish retreat design for a Day of Healing with the elderly, homebound, and infirm from a parish. The design ended up being shrunk from a daylong event to an afternoon because of the health limitations of those invited. Ample time had to be left between sessions so that ambulatory issues could be negotiated with the limited number of rest rooms and stairs. Increasingly, we are becoming sensitive to the need to take into account the special concerns of the disabled. These factors must be integrated into the overall scheduling of a retreat, day of recollection, or formation event.

These issues can surprise us and complicate our design if we do not anticipate them. A planning team should meet and brainstorm as many of the issues that the audience may have so as to be as prepared as possible. The schedule is then less likely to be tampered with and all those involved will feel like they know what is going on and when everything is supposed to happen. This provides greater security for all those attending.

Strategy Four:
Structural Design

As a junior in high school, I first identified with Christ on a parish retreat. My particular experience of adolescent rejection was one which drew me to the crucifixion of Christ. However, as if this wasn't powerful enough, on that same retreat I learned that others at times had experiences much more difficult than I. I will never forget the school football hero telling us, through tears, how he had found his sister...after she had committed suicide. Retreats seem to provide an important time for teens to open themselves to a different type of relationship with Jesus.

—J. V., PASTORAL PLANNER

When we speak of the structural design of a retreat, we are referring to the individual input sessions that make up the substance and content that serve as the retreat's focus. In a retreat setting, that which is formative allows us to connect with ourselves, our God, and each other. With that basis, the structure must reflect a balance that allows for that "connecting" to happen organically. When planning a retreat, it is essential that we *create a time and a space for prayer and reflection* that is both formative and informative. As has been mentioned, structural design is significantly connected with the overall schedule and format phase. The entire schedule reflects within a larger time-frame the balance of formative aspects and informative content. When we speak of the structural design of the retreat, we are speaking of the main thrust of the content that will be presented. Input sessions, lectures, and reflections are all means by which we try to get a point across to the retreatants. Therefore, a balance of the following six elements strengthens the structural design of individual input sessions, as well as enhancing the schedule and format of the whole retreat:

- Informative and Inspirational
- Active and Contemplative
- Solitude and Solidarity

Informative and Inspirational

During a retreat, input is usually given to guide the retreatants. This input can be informative; it can also be inspirational. Formation can happen in the interface between information and inspiration.

Information can be disseminated to a group in a number of different ways. Lecture, video, and dialogue are common forms. Input can also be given in provocative ways that stimulate reflection, questions, and conversation. Activities that prompt participants to think again about something often provide a rich opportunity for "unpacking" feelings, thoughts, and reactions in a small group. Music and lyrics can convey meaning and provide a challenge to the listener in a novel way.

Inspiration (*in-spira*), the breathing of the Holy Spirit into us, moves the familiar into a new light. We may have already known the "information" given, but the way in which it is now presented gives new meaning and vibrancy to the ideas. We take it up in a different way. With inspiration, the Holy Spirit moves on the natural inclination of hearts towards awe and wonder. Material that is presented with "inspiration" in mind prepares the human heart for that organic movement.

Therefore, input needs to be presented with a fresh twist. It needs to incorporate a new slant for us to ponder. It needs to present something for our consideration that turns us on our ear and makes us think through it further, pray through it more deliberately, and listen to it more attentively. Input is a word spoken to us that stirs us inside and predisposes us to inspiration. Whether the input is primarily informational or not, to be effective it must be delivered creatively and reflectively in a retreat setting. This can be a major challenge to planners, but one which is well worth their while, especially when working on youth retreats, sacramental preparation, or parish retreats where the participants may be present under some obligation.

Active and Contemplative

A retreat which is composed strictly of passive listening to a speaker is likely to fall flat as far as having an enduring impact on the retreatants. Especially when dealing with youth or young adults, active components must be woven into the retreat design. Activity that is formative can be as simple as participative dialogue. It can be engaging the group in a question-and-answer process or asking for examples from retreatants' lives that illustrate the relevance of the content. Games, physical movement, and sharing are all activities that lend excitement to otherwise anesthetic, monologue-based retreats. Preached retreats have greater power when they incorporate some active elements.

Information may be inspirational, but for the dissemination of information to become "formative," planners need to keep in mind that the retreatants need time for assimilation. Time is needed to hear the information being given and to register the content. Time is also needed for that information to sink down inside the hearer and move from a cognitive level to one of the heart.

This is the contemplative aspect of retreat time. This "heart time" takes longer than the "head time." For real digestion, a slowed down atmosphere is more helpful and conducive for promoting a contemplative way of being.

Inspiration also deserves some "savoring time." It tastes so sweet that we want to chew on it a bit longer. This may call us to write in a journal, pray over a given scriptural text, or wander contemplatively in a private place and let it penetrate more fully. Abbreviating this savoring can flip us into a functional mode and thwart a rich opportunity for a deepening in faith and personal integration.

Formation can occur when we are moved on some level by something that is going on during the retreat. The possibility for inspiration to occur is fundamentally in the hands of the Holy Spirit. But in the design of the retreat, we as planners can use what we have found to be moving for us to set the stage for those for whom we plan.

Therefore, in designing an experience that is meant to be spiritually formative, it is helpful to structure the sessions for the retreatants, blending a combination of active and contemplative elements. Creative forms of delivering the message, combined with active elements supporting it, will grab the attention of retreatants. Surrounding the input there should be ample time for reflection, sharing, quiet time, and prayer to deepen that attentiveness.

Solitude and Solidarity

To further develop the contemplative dimension in a retreat, solitude is essential. Many people automatically associate the term "retreat" with solitude. It is a worthy association, one which most people secretly crave but may not know how to facilitate in their daily life. Times of solitude within the retreat structure overtly give people permission to take that for which they are starved. It provides a supportive structure in which they can slow down and enter into a deeper level of awareness. Solitude can be frightening for many, as they are unaccustomed to gearing down and entering their own interiority, but when periods of reflection are offered with some helpful focus to ground the retreatant, the fear of solitude can diminish and be overcome.

Solitude is typically associated with retreat experience, but solidarity is an equally important element in the design structure of contemporary retreats. There is a growing awareness that spiritual processes do not merely serve the individual in his or her personal transformation. It is no longer an era with a strictly "me and Jesus" spirituality. While on retreat the element of solidarity ties the individual back into a larger community.

Within the input itself, the mention of the larger world and our contribution to its formation and transformation can engender a greater awareness of how crucial solidarity is. Solidarity implies many tiers of relationship. The Church is a global community lived out locally, but it must not be forgotten that the Body of Christ extends beyond provincial and parochial boundaries. It is important to raise the consciousness of those attending the retreat, drawing their attention to this relationship and linking them up more responsibly with others when they depart.

Solidarity is also an element which opens the door for the surrounding community to contribute to the retreat process. The community framework may be the larger body of the parish, the diocese, or the regional community. It may be the family to whom the retreatant returns following the retreat. In consciously questioning where solidarity is evidenced in the retreat and following it, the enrichment of the retreat can be felt beyond the retreat doors.

One way of allowing solidarity to emerge within the larger community, who pray beyond the walls of the retreat for the retreatants, is to design a closing session which incorporates the families, friends, and parents of those attending. The Cursillo Movement (at the heart of which is a specialized, three-day retreat program) does an excellent job of this in their structural design. The closing of each retreat becomes richer when a session or prayer service ties the time apart to those who await the return of the retreatant.

Structuring in a "return component" for the retreatants is a helpful plus that reconnects them with the community from whom they have come. Especially for youth, this "welcome upon return" is important. Another final touch can be a "welcome party" sponsored by other youth for the returnees at the end of a retreat. This allows for some further "processing" and a more graceful reintegration into the family, the parish, or the youth group. It also raises the awareness of those at home that this retreat has occurred and support for ongoing spiritual nurturing needs to continue. Reunions after retreat are also powerful ways to extend the vitality experienced during retreat to later life.

These three sets of polarities of information and inspiration, active and contemplative, and solitude and solidarity can enrich the structural design of the input sessions and worship component of a retreat. It is less important to plan an abundance of activities with many ideas ricocheting throughout the retreat period than to deliver a simple, focused, and balanced presentation that provides food for thought and prayer. Dazzling the retreatants with a plethora of thoughts is not ideal on a retreat. The adage "less is best" is one that should be listened to when a proliferation of good ideas erupts in planning. Focusing the sessions and limiting the images is essential for quality experience, one that allows for the spontaneity of the Holy Spirit in the quiet time.

Selections From a Retreat Sampler

One effective format for input sessions in planning retreats, especially for youth or young adults, is a structure that incorporates the following:

- Activity
- Reflection
- Quiet time/Journal time
- Polling time/Brainstorm
- Sharing time
- Input
- Prayer

An *activity* can be any provocative process that prompts a call to reflect and think again. Effective activities which can be used are:

- Role-plays (particularly effective for youth and adults)
- Games (an icebreaker game; a trust game)
- Simulations (poverty simulations; global meals; war games)
- Guided meditations (use imagination for prayer encounters)
- Musical pieces of meaning (print the lyrics so they can be read by the listeners)

Ideally, the *activity* is selected by the planners specifically for a spiritual or theological message which can be derived from it. The planning team may have decided on a theme and then brainstormed approaches to illustrating that idea. In dialogue and creative interplay, ideas for a suitable activity that could setup the input can be designed. We as planners can refine the activity around the emphasis we want to make in the input portion of the session.

Just as the planning team may have needed time to tease out the meaning of the activity, so the retreatants can be encouraged to do the same within the session. There are many ways to invite participants into the reflective process of making these connections. Sharing verbally their reactions or responses to the activity can generate further associations and meanings for the whole group. A skilled facilitator or a staff member may:

- help *massage the associations that come up in the group* and write them up quickly on butcher paper as they are spoken out without editing;
- *invite the group to silence,* especially following a thoughtful piece of music or a role-play;
- encourage reflection through *writing in a journal* for fifteen minutes;
- *take a poll* to obtain the reactions of the group and then brainstorm the meanings they derive.

The person who will give the input has already ascertained what some of these responses might be through careful reflection and brainstorming with the retreat planners. This person can then tease out some of the ramifications of these meanings and move the group in a direction that weaves in other aspects of wisdom. For youth and young adults, keeping the input to eight to ten minutes prevents unnecessary verbosity and allows for a succinct focus for their continued reflection. A pause following the input can be given for quiet or continued writing in journals or breaking into dyads, triads, and small groups for further integration.

Finally, a prayer ritual incorporating music, sacred gesture, Scripture or sacred reading, quiet, and other pertinent actions can be designed to enhance the input. The ritual takes the input into the context of prayer and communal worship. It slows down the receiving of the word and the digesting of it. A pertinent piece of music may further illustrate the point. Perhaps replaying a musical piece that was used earlier will take the reflection deeper when it is set up well with Scripture, another spiritual text, or a special gesture. Leave ample time for quiet in which retreatants may breathe in the contemplative space. Close with the peace rite and a song to be sung together in a circle or with hands held.

Notes From the Author

This format can be utilized in the time frame of an evening, a day, or a weekend. I have seen it very effectively used as the structure for a week-long youth leadership camp. I have also used it for youth gatherings of just three hours in length. A meal often followed these sessions so that there was more social time than the design would have otherwise allowed. While this is particularly appropriate for younger persons, it is not totally inappropriate for older adults. Few of us really listen well beyond ten minutes of a lecture. There is a tendency for the listeners to primarily use their reasoning ability ("flip up into their heads") and miss out on the affective nudge by the Holy Spirit. Taking notes in order to remember helps the duration of our attention, but on retreat few do so.

Therefore, planners will need to repeat major themes throughout the retreat. Be careful not to use too many symbols, especially on a short retreat. Layering images is much more effective. In the first session, start with the image of the seed, then add the idea of soil in the next session. Complement these with water, and so forth, and build a unified image that is interconnected and not too heavy with contrary symbolism. Let the "centerspot"—as spoken of in the section on setup and ambiance—build with each agricultural image. Don't be afraid to repeat ideas or embellish images.

Strategy Five:
Setup and Ambiance

The building and grounds very much had a medieval feel to them. The church bell was rung at each of the offices of the day. I loved the reminder of the call to prayer.... The whole place lent itself to silence, reflection, and prayer. As I walked from the retreat house to the chapel for vigils, I felt enshrouded by the night mist. The silence was enormous and I reveled in it.

—M. L. V., LITURGY PLANNER AND MOTHER OF FOUR

Setup and ambiance, the fifth "S" strategy, is about "creating space" for people to encounter the Holy. It is the creative incarnation of all the planning and preparation leading up to the actual event. It can become one of the most enjoyable and playful phases because we put our creativity into form by creating "ambiance." In this fifth phase, we are basically asking ourselves one question:

• How do we create sacred space?

This is a key question. If attention is not paid to the ambiance and the layout of the retreat environment, much can be forfeited with regard to the extra effectiveness of that goal. The space that we are providing for the retreatant must be one that is conducive to the intimate encounter with God that we want to facilitate. The atmosphere of the retreat space ushers the retreatants into this intimacy. They should not have to fight distractions exacerbated by the environment to have a good experience.

It may also be desirable that the space be a place of meaningful encounter with other participants. Therefore, there may be several concerns to keep in mind when creating sacred space. As retreat planners, it is necessary that we pay attention to the atmosphere that helps or hinders those we serve. Lack of planning is not helpful in the long run.

Here details come into play. It is often in the details that the refinement of a retreat plan and sensitivity to what helps people pray is seen. Let us ask ourselves these questions as planners:

- What helps us pray? What helps us focus?

The answers to these questions can tune us in to what subtle and obvious externals facilitate the prayer process of others. Answers that come to mind include:

- Quiet space, dimly lit
- Soft music, like Gregorian chant or classical instrumental flute
- A beautiful natural environment
- Candlelight
- Uncluttered, open space
- A prominent crucifix or symbolic picture

These answers provide the planner with information about how to create a sacred space. Obviously, in a group experience, all of the individual idiosyncratic preferences cannot be realized. However, in general, we can provide a thoughtful space for most people to find some degree of ease.

Greater care has to be paid to the arrangement of furniture, decor, and reserved reflection space, that is, the chapel or oratory, when working with a group. Symbols and decor can enhance or deter the focus of a group significantly. Once the retreat has begun special attention to the transitions into prayer, silence, and reflection can enhance the creation of an internal space as well. First, let us consider some basics.

The Basics

Some basic human wisdoms should always be taken into account when facilitating the prayer process. We know them already from having been in groups where they *weren't* sufficiently addressed and, as a result, we found ourselves distracted or uncomfortable. Common sense tells us to be attentive to:

- The *temperature* of the room—not too hot (which induces drowsiness), and not too cold (which the retreatant has to defend against).
- *Comfort*—is the furniture comfortable, attractive, and suitable for the retreat purpose?
- *Facilitators*—can they be heard and seen? Do they have suitable supplies for illustrations and amplification, if necessary?
- The *noise level*—if we want a reflective atmosphere, diminish outside noises and the use of those materials (for example, radios, headsets, and so forth) that impair the attentiveness of the listeners.

In addition, there should be sufficient room for the size of the group that we hope to host. Furniture should be arranged in groupings that facilitate the process to which we are inviting the retreatants. If small group discussion is desired, cluster chairs or arrange movable chairs in semicircular rows that can be easily turned to form groups of two and three. To promote solitude, arrange chairs with plenty of space around them, facing the speaker.

If writing is a part of the process, secure tables or create open floor space with pillows for comfort upon which people can lean and prop themselves. Always keep in mind the age of the participants when planning "floor" use. Most people over forty do not appreciate or feel comfortable sitting on a floor for any length of time, but many adolescents prefer it.

Important Pluses—"Warming Up the Place"

Most of us are alert enough to know what helps us "feel at home" and what doesn't. In a retreat, "feeling at home" is an underlying objective that aids the participants in feeling comfortable and at ease. As mentioned, attention to detail distinguishes the sophisticated planner from the novice. Transforming neutral space into a "welcoming" space—"warming up the place"—is an important skill.

Often retreat houses have been converted from old convents, schools, or institutional buildings. Warming them up can diminish the associations that such buildings provoke. A variety of means can be used to make a building or room more user-friendly, including:

- Soft lighting
- Greenery and plants
- Music
- Furnishing arrangements
- Art and symbols

Soft Lighting

Soft lighting can create an ambiance that slows people down and predisposes them to a more contemplative orientation. Lamps provide a warmer glow than overhead fluorescent lights, which often hum and give off irritating vibrations. If the ambiance that is desired is quieter and focused, pull the drapes shut. If the outside atmosphere is naturally inspiring, situate the furniture in such a way that the beauty is highlighted in keeping with the retreat objective.

Candlelight can be very effective for creating sacred space, using such lighting in chapels and oratories. Always place a candle on a noninflammable base that can catch the drips and, if possible, surround them with a glass chimney or the like. A single candle for prayer can help a group center. Equally enchanting is to walk into a room lit with votive lights. The effect is an almost instantaneous awareness that "this is sacred space."

Greenery and Plants

Greenery and plants soften a sterile environment and warm it up. Clustering plants in corners or using plants to section off a part of the room can serve as creative ways to decorate without importing excessive imagery. An arrangement in front of the podium used by the speaker or greenery on each table can add color without being obtrusive.

Music

Music can warm up the atmosphere. Arriving to soft, subdued instrumental music can often soothe a group immediately and invite them to enter into this space differently than others. Selections that are age-appropriate and situationally effective do a great deal to acclimate a group to the focus of the retreat.

If separate space is available for a chapel, a soft undercurrent of chant or harp can facilitate a group moving into "internal sacred space." Many churches today pipe in select recorded music for visitors' benefit in an attempt to help them pause graciously. On retreat, music can initially help people make the transition from "the marketplace of life" to the "inner sanctum" with God. After some time, music can fade out slowly and people will be more able to rest in their own stillness.

Furnishing Arrangements

Furnishing arrangements physically structure the space for the events of the retreat. The spatial arrangement of chairs and tables, decorated with tablecloths, tells the retreatant something about the expectations of the retreat team. Arranging situational gathering spaces in cozy clusters can warm up a group. If conversation or discussion within groups is planned, arrange chairs in the room in small circles or semicircles. A casual environment facilitates conversation and relaxation. Pillows on the floor with low tables and comfortable chairs give a different message.

Knowing the objectives for different portions of the retreat and creating appropriate space for each of these can highly influence the effectiveness of the retreat. Do not be afraid to rearrange the space between events within the retreat in order to accommodate a different focus. Changing the space can get the attention of the retreatant, especially adolescents, in a way that refreshes their focus.

Art and Symbols

Art and symbols can reinforce the retreat themes when done tastefully and deliberately. Color, fabric, and pictures can evoke a response from retreatants. A drape of fabric for the liturgical season can connect the retreat to the larger liturgical life of the Church. Select artistic, evocative, or reflective photographs can also help. In retreats where groups are reporting back information that was generated in small groups, allow them to record their thoughts on newsprint and use these as decorations to remind the group of the process they have been engaged in throughout the duration of the retreat.

Using a symbol throughout the retreat and duplicating it on initial mailings, retreat schedules, handouts, and as a gift during a closing ritual can carry the theme throughout the entire experience.

Special Touches

The extra touch of artistic minds and hands can make a great impact on a retreatant. The following "special touches" are some "extras" that have worked for others.

Centerspots

Create a "centerspot" whenever prayer or reflection is desired in the group. Drape a small table in cloth and place it in a central spot in the room with chairs configured around it. Use candles, a picture, a photo, or a word that symbolizes some aspect of the retreat, and arrange a plant or flowers around that. This helps anchor the group on key words or images throughout the retreat. Even if a retreatant doesn't remember all of the input, they may remember "that picture." It is also helpful for centering prayer periods. Focus the light on that centerspot with a spotlight or intensity lamp and dim the rest of the lights. Retreatants will naturally set their eyes on the image highlighted.

Musical Interludes

Use of music for reflection and prayer can be an excellent enhancement to a speaker or to creating ambiance. Crucial, however, is the way that music is introduced and eliminated. Important: turning off the music must be done with the awareness that abruptness jars the listener. It is startling to have music shut off in the middle of the song or to hear the loud click of the player at the end of a meditation. Phasing out the music gradually by turning down the volume, and then muffling the stop switch can do much to maintain the ambiance of quiet and reverence and extend the reflectiveness. Better yet, use the pause button on the cassette player. CD players are even more desirable in that they allow for the quick selection of a piece, starting it and stopping it without extra noise. Be conscientious about these details.

Closing Rituals

Designing a ritual for the closing that includes a gift to take home can extend the time of the retreat. The gift can be as simple as a "diploma" wrapped in ribbon with the names and addresses of each of the retreatants for contact later. A candle or symbol from the retreat that can be understood in light of the retreat experience is a wonderful treasure to return to in prayer afterwards. These thoughtful touches remind the retreatant of the formative experience and their intention to take it further.

Selections From a Retreat Sampler

The following resources are possibilities that can enhance the setup and ambiance of a retreat:

Music

- Chant has become popular again with all age groups. It is a very effective way to suggest "sacred space" to people. Try "Hildegard von Bingen: 11,000 Virgins," performed by Anonymous 4.
- Classical Recordings such as Pachelbel's Canon in D and selected recordings by contemporary musicians may also be effective. James Galway's flute instrumentals are suitable for creating an ambiance. Oboe, cello, violin, and harpsichord can also be good surrounding music. Chamber music of most forms can create a quiet atmosphere.
- Contemporary vocalists and instrumentals can provide soothing strains for creating ambiance. Enya, a female vocalist with instrumentals, is very effective as is some of the alternative music available, for example, Kitaro, Paul Winter, George Winston, and John Tesh.
- Religious music is always a possibility. Recordings by many of the current liturgical writers are available through different liturgical publishing groups. GIA and OCP have seasonal religious recordings and comprehensive collections of the music which is sung within many pastoral contexts, including an extensive collection of the psalms. Catalogs are available upon request:

GIA 1-800-GIA-1358
Oregon Catholic Press (OCP) 1-800-LITURGY

- There are also scripturally-based musicians who use the psalms, the epistles, and biblical metaphors for their lyrics. John Michael Talbot has produced ample pieces very suitable for reflection and contemplative prayer. For youth and young adult retreats, there is a large volume of Christian rock music available on CD with very appropriate lyrics. Christian musicians like Amy Grant, Michael Card,

Rich Mullins, Michelle Tumes, and Terry Talbot are only a few whose music can be incorporated.

Art

- Icons are very popular these days as centering images. Use these for centerspots, but also shrink them and duplicate them for the cover of worship leaflets or as a logo on schedules and handouts.
- Landscapes, waterscapes, and mountains can reinforce biblical themes.
- Greeting cards of a contemporary or classical theme can be made into a centerspot. Classical possibilities include Matisse's "Icarus" and Maxfield Parrish's "Ecstasy." The "creation touch" of God and Adam in Michelangelo's painting in the Sistine Chapel is also powerful.

Notes From the Author

Setup and ambiance possibilities are only limited by the creativity of the planners. Be open to finding photographs or music in unlikely places, for example, on greeting cards from friends, from a teenager's collection of music, and from nature. For logos, check out a "clip art" package or computer program for possibilities. These are easy to duplicate onto notices and handouts to carry the theme visually.

The following tips will help with preparing an ambiance that maximizes the impact of the retreat:

1. Visit the site before the day of your use. Forewarned is forearmed. Knowing the site in advance, you can layout a floor plan and bring with you commodities that could help you.
2. Bring extra supplies that you know could help create sacred space. You don't have to use them all, but you are prepared for the possibility.

3. Get to your site *early*. A minimum of two hours gives you ample time check out the limits of the building, gather your team and systematically create your space. It also allows you time as a team to calm down after setting up and focus yourselves.

4. Gather your team for prayer before your retreatants arrive. This helps ground the entire group on the purpose of the retreat and gives you a good foundation together.

CHAPTER THREE

Special Areas of Concern in Creating Parish Retreats

~

Being on retreat allows the space and time to hush the
constant stream of discursive thought coursing through
my mind. It is like an extended prayer, where I can actively listen to God and more fully explore and experience his grace. In a materialistic and ego-driven society, it
is encouraging to observe and spend time with others as
they travel along their own spiritual road. For me, retreats
have been a way to remember who I am fundamentally
and spiritually.

—M. K. G., EUCHARISTIC MINISTER AND
OFFICE MANAGER

The five planning and design strategies outlined in the first portion of this manual provide basic structures for planners in preparing for a small group retreat. However, to really deepen and
embellish the retreat process, we as planners have to take into account further means to make the experience spiritually formative.
There are additional areas of concern that are especially important
in helping us as planners take our preparations to a deeper, more
creative and spiritually enriching level. This second section of our
manual addresses four of those special areas of concern: the use of
metaphors around which a retreat can be planned, the complementarity
of creative worship and liturgy, helpful evaluation tools for team
feedback, and the necessity of self-care for the retreat director.

Each of these four special areas of concern further enhance the planning done within the initial five strategy stages. The spiritual need and scriptural grounding strategies are directly addressed in the use of creative metaphors and the communal worship component of a retreat. Creative metaphors from Scripture, poetry, or nature provide concrete symbols which can help retreatants tease out the meanings and associations that are being presented by the facilitators. Planners can stimulate the memories of the participants visually and artistically by replicating the images conjured up by the metaphors in the setup and ambiance of the environment. Jesus himself used many metaphors in his preaching to help illustrate his points ("The kingdom of heaven is like...."). Retreat planners can maximize the imagination of the retreatants by employing a similar practice and using art to illustrate their points and trigger the imagination further.

Evaluation tools provide concrete feedback to planners about all five of the initial strategies. Through structured evaluation, planners can determine how effective their designs were, clarifying if the scheduling and format, structural design, and setup and ambiance components of the retreat supported the retreatants in their spiritual process, as well as if people's needs were met.

Finally, the self-care of the retreat director is an often overlooked component that, if ignored, can result in depletion and exhaustion. This final chapter outlines six basic spiritual formation tips for keeping the spiritual vitality of retreat directors alive. We as planners often neglect our own inner life by overextending ourselves or defending our work as one that is prayerful in nature, even if it cuts into our personal prayer time. This omission can have serious consequences. To assure that as much longevity as possible is maintained among retreat teams, we must attend to our own self-care and spiritual nourishment.

Each of the additional areas of concern can greatly enhance the initial planning. They can enrich the experience of the retreatants and provide greater inspiration for the team and participants alike.

The Use of Metaphors
in Creating Retreats

Each retreat that I have shared in has allowed me to hear a special word from the Lord. There has always been some touch, some word for the moment, some special knowing or mercy that I have received by going on retreat. Initially, attending retreats was an in-filling experience—a time to renew, look inward, listen, and then move outward.... In serving on retreat, I find the experience of pouring out linked closely with the in-filling sensation. While giving and offering myself to those on retreat, I found the Lord more than responsive to my own needs and hungers. The perception of being a "hollow reed" through which the life-giving energy flows to the plant is the picture in my mind's eye of my life and the power, love, and mercy of Jesus to my fellow retreatants.

—C. A. F., PARAMEDIC AND CHILDREN'S CHOIR DIRECTOR

Some of the most powerful retreat experiences people recall revolve around the memory of a symbol. An image took on new meaning during a lecture, a prayer service, or liturgy during the retreat. Selecting a single potent image to refer to throughout the retreat gives the retreatants time to look at the symbol in a new light, dwell with it, and distill new associations. This, of course, requires the selection of an effective symbol or image that has many layers of meaning and potential. Scripture is filled with such images. Imagination and visualization are key faculties that can lead us to new insights and connections.

Metaphor and Symbol

In the Italian film, *Il Postino* ("The Postman"), Mario Ruopollo seeks counsel from the great Chilean poet, Pablo Neruda, who is in exile in Italy. Mario, a semi-illiterate postman, is most impressed with Neruda's impact on women and he beseeches Neruda to teach him the secret to winning a woman's heart. Neruda reveals the richness of "metaphors" to Mario, inviting him to see the rich images of his own land, his life, and the woman he loves through appreciative eyes. The world of symbol and analogy introduces Mario to his own innate poetic capacities and wisdom.

We are tactile people. We are impressed by those things that we can touch and see. Based on the context in which we perceive things, we remember them and create associations around them. They become meaningful to us, taking on a significance that continues to enrich our lives.

Retreats are prime periods of time for meaning-making. Placed in the rarified environment of prayer and communal support, images can take on new vitality and power. An image can focus our attention and then invite our imagination to creatively extend our understanding of it. Retreat directors can utilize this opportunity by weaving in pertinent symbols to further embellish the retreat experience for the retreatants.

The Use of Scriptural Images in Retreat Designs

Primary sources for religious imagery and spiritual nuance are the Hebrew Scriptures and the New Testament. When looking at the means to seize the attention of retreatants, we often look to the powerful symbols within the Gospels. The Bible is rich in images from everyday life which are not exclusive to first century Palestine. The Gospels are full of references which can be employed in building a design, such as banquets, healings, and conversions. When crafting a design for a retreat, it is helpful to identify images from Scripture that are multi-dimensional and can be layered potently throughout the retreat.

There are many ways to tease out a metaphor or an image with our retreat planners. One method for doing so is to select a pertinent text and begin brainstorming, surfacing the associations that naturally come forth from the text. Without editing the group, freely expound on the connections that are made from the specific text.

Let the group assemble as many spin-offs from the original image which come readily to mind. Allow them to explain their associations after the brainstorming has finished. Let further associations be added if they arise. Then begin to organize the ideas in ways that allow the images to illustrate the theme of the retreat.

As an example, the metaphor used in the parable of the Great Dinner (Lk 14:15–24) may generate images of eating, celebrating, being invited, resisting invitation, obstacles to participation, preparedness, feeding each other, reaching out, inclusiveness, justice, and so forth. Gradually, a text takes on greater meaning among the planners, and avenues for interpretation and expansion emerge. How can these themes be progressively built upon to effectively lead a group into a new understanding of the text and its application in their lives? Each input session is an opportunity to specifically focus the retreatants on another facet of the text and relate it to their everyday lives.

Another way to tease out a metaphor is to use a concordance, to list as many references to specific images in the Bible as may be pertinent. Choose a primary symbol like "oil" or "light," gather the references, and see what themes and associations occur from these references. Do they open a new course of direction for us as retreat planners? Which texts seem as if they would be more significant to those for whom we are specifically planning?

For example, for elderly retreatants, texts from Isaiah's "suffering servant" chapters, referring to comfort and strengthening feeble hands, may be most fitting for a healing service within the retreat. In their own twilight, the elderly may need comfort to face the waning of skills and abilities. Adolescents, on the other hand, may tune in to "a light shines in the darkness," and the retreat team could devise ways to utilize light and symbolize its many forms meaningfully for youth who are struggling in the darkness of puberty and peer pressure. The planners can layer the retreat with different experiences of light and darkness, using daylight, evening light, midnight light, and candlelight to illustrate the passage from darkness to light.

Symbols that affect people the most powerfully are often those that are primal, such as the symbols used in our liturgical life. Light and dark, fire, food, oil, water, and touch are universal images that permeate scriptural texts. The use of these create visual centerspots that can be added creatively during the retreat to anchor the group's imagination and give them visual references to remember.

When we design a retreat, we may want to ask questions such as:

- What images from Scripture come to mind as we connect with the theme that we would like to introduce?
- Are there specific stories that come up in our knowledge of Scripture that seem meaningful in relation to the theme of our retreat?
- How could we creatively highlight this image to get our message across (music, symbols, centerspots, lighting, and so forth)?
- Can this image be used within the worship portions of the retreat as well?

From these personal associations, the primal images can be identified and developed. The group can begin to discuss how to highlight the image, refining it and adjusting it as each new group demands. Each group's individual enthusiasm and associations for the image will guide their creative use of the symbol.

An example which may be helpful comes from the classic parable of the Prodigal Son. The returning child, the forgiving parent, the jealous sibling are images that we all can relate to. Each of these calls us to examine the narrowness of our lives and identify where we need to be stretched. An entire retreat could focus around these three figures and invite us to identify where we resonate with each figure. How do we relate to each character? A centerspot could feature a pair of sandals pointing away for the younger son, placed on top of flowing cloth with greenery around it. The father could be depicted with a cane or staff, propped against a tree stump or old chair. The older brother could be represented with a ring of keys or another pair of shoes remaining at a distance. The parable could be read during the closing liturgy and built into a final reflection on reconciliation, return, and homecoming.

Metaphors are rich, multi-tiered images that can evoke reflection. Utilizing these symbols and representing them visually in forms that provoke thought, we as retreat planners can open new dimensions for those we serve. Simple, yet profound, scriptural metaphors teach and capture our imagination repeatedly. Perhaps Jesus knew what he was doing in using so many concrete images to instruct the many generations which would flock to him throughout time.

Selections From a Retreat Sampler

Most vividly, the parables of Jesus provide ample imagery for embellishment when planning retreats. Seemingly mundane objects and situations can become rich in new interpretation when a retreat team teases out further nuance for the participants. Decor can feature and highlight these objects in centerspots for visual reminders. Surrounded by candles and set apart, these objects take on new significance. Following the retreat, participants may find themselves captivated repeatedly at Mass or in prayer when they hear the images proclaimed again in Scripture.

To stimulate our reflection, ten scriptural images, mostly from the New Testament, have been provided below with their textual references. A few reflective questions are provided to stimulate the development of their thematic use for the structural design strategy or for prayer. Each of these could be illustrated with concrete symbols in a centerspot. These are further developed in the section, "Worship and Liturgy in Retreats" (p. 72).

- "the seed" (Mt 13:3–9): What is the seed inside me that is trying to germinate? Is the soil of my life, my interior (spiritual) life and my exterior actions, helping that seed to grow and develop?
- "the feeding" (Mt 14:13–21): What do I have to share with God's people that I am clinging to and not sharing? Why?

Do I believe there is bounty and abundance in Christ? Can I trust that? Will I let him feed me?

- "the forgiving parent" (Lk 15:11–32): Who do I relate to in this story? Why? Have I ever experienced the benevolent embrace of God like this? Who do I hold grudges against in my life?

- "the withered hand" (Mt 12:9–14): What is withered up inside of me right now? Do I know my preciousness before God? Do I recognize preciousness in others?

- "the net" (Mt 13:47–52): In my net, what sorts of things have I collected? What helps me in my spiritual journey? What hinders me? What old and new treasures from Church history can I bring from my storeroom to enrich me?

- "the salt of the earth" (Mt 5:13): How am I the salt that gives life to others? What is the salt I offer? Has my inner life gone flat? What would restore it?

- "the light of the world" (Mt 5:14–16): Am I living under a bushel basket? How? Is my goodness seen by others? Is it shining through me? Where?

- "the storm at sea" (Lk 8:22–25): What are the storms inside that are preoccupying me? Can I slow down and allow God to enter my storm? Where is my faith? Where is my courage?

- "hidden treasure" (Mt 13:44): What is the buried treasure within my community? Why are we hiding it? Is Christ worth giving all that I have?

Using Metaphors in Retreat Designs: Questions

Use the following questions to surface scriptural images, metaphors, and passages.

- Are there stories that come to mind in our knowledge of Scripture that seem meaningful in relation to our theme?

- What images from Scripture come up to mind as we connect with the theme that we would like to introduce?
- How could we creatively highlight these images to get our message across (music, symbols, centerspots, lighting, and so forth)?
- Can these images be used within the worship portions of the retreat as well?

Worship and Liturgy in Retreats

I believe worship is incredibly vital to a retreat because as a participant and as a leader I have witnessed the change and transformation of people's hearts to the true and living presence of God. People are more open when they are singing; they go from a spirit of just being there to entering the throne room of grace.

—A. M. S., MEDICAL TECHNOLOGIST
AND CHILDREN'S HOMILIST

We can be so attentive to planning the input and facilitating sessions in a retreat that we miss out on a significant "formative" opportunity for those assembled: worship. Incredibly significant within retreat contexts is the actual prayer-time together. In this chapter, we will examine the place of worship and prayer within small group retreats. Worship and prayer are complemented by the other five strategies, as well as serving as a locus for the further exploration of metaphors from sacred Scripture.

The Value of Worship and Prayer in a Group Retreat

Many times when retreatants are asked to reflect on their experience after a retreat to ascertain what was most moving for them, what they cite as most significant was the opportunity to pray together. While they may recall some of the general information given during the group sessions and the teachings offered, well-planned and well-orchestrated worship can have the greatest impact of all. Why is this so?

People who go on retreat know they are entering into sacred territory. They understand that a retreat is a place of encounter with God. They are stepping onto sacred ground. Like Moses, they sense that it is appropriate to remove their shoes, to divest themselves of some defensive stance that shields them from a naked moment with

God. It is a charged environment and time. Their expectations shift with this awareness. Even if much of this is unconscious, the expectation of the Holy has caused a stir in them.

Often underlying this awareness is a hidden desire to somehow meet God in a different way. Grace may have already played a role in readying them for this possibility. Even if there is some obvious resistance, they may have been subtly groomed for a glance into the mystery of God. Since most of us on some primordial level hunger for this, the experience of retreat becomes an opportunity for a heightened sensitivity to the touch of God.

Father Armand Nigro, a Jesuit retreat master from Gonzaga University in Spokane, Washington, used to say that, while on retreat, people's awareness of God was so elevated that someone could read them the telephone book and they would get something out of it. While his comments may more specifically be referring to adults in an extended private retreat, many youth and young adults are comparably attuned on a deeper level to the movement of God in this sacred time. Even if they cannot articulate it, they organically know a hunger for something more, a hunger for the divine mystery of God.

Therefore, it is essential that we as retreat planners take very seriously the partnership we enter into in preparing the opportunities for worship and prayer in this special time. We want to highlight and assist in the encounter, not deter or force it. We want to facilitate a gentle meeting between God and the vulnerable or—perhaps—defensive retreatant. Then, we can step back and let God do the work that only the Spirit can do.

This heightened sensitivity among the retreatants is one reason to plan carefully the worship element of the retreat. Other valuable reasons to attend to the prayer portions of the retreat include the following:

- Worship and liturgy can highlight themes and related issues that complement the facilitator's input.
- Communal prayer becomes a meaningful place for

retreatants to pull together their private prayer and join others in solidarity.
- Within a retreat context, creative forms of prayer can be utilized more effectively than in more restricted situations.

Theme-Building Through Liturgy

Theme-building requires relating the liturgical portion of the retreat to the content and focus of the event in an appropriate way. Most of us as retreat planners would never think of excluding structured prayer in common from the retreat design. We already recognize the formative opportunity that worship affords us in a retreat context. The planning of the liturgical events within the retreat requires a good awareness of the goals and objectives identified for the whole spiritual event.

Private Prayer Linked in Solidarity

Many retreatants live busy lives which inhibit their practice of private prayer. They look to retreat times for a restoration of their private prayer. They come seeking nourishment for their souls. Quiet, reflective time for them is an essential component for a meaningful retreat experience.

However, if retreat merely fosters a private devotion without linking it to the larger human and global community, it may not be doing all that it is intended to do. Retreat should foster a greater sense of connectedness with creation as well as with the Creator. A grounded sense of solidarity—through which the gospel mandate is expressed as care and concern for the larger created reality—is very important.

Whether it is eucharistic or noneucharistic, attention must be paid to the communal worship that ties us to the larger Body of Christ. Communal worship during retreat affords each individual an opportunity to link their prayer with that of the whole. It is powerful to witness many unique souls coming together to join their hearts and minds in prayer, with a common focus and a mutual willingness. Joined together in prayer, people can experience an even greater solidarity with one another. They can also tap into the powerful support that communal prayer provides. Many hearts praying together generates a very special energy that differs from praying alone. Liturgy and worship during retreat facilitates this dynamic.

Creative Forms of Prayer

Within the normal parish context, communal prayer is often limited to Sunday Eucharist, periodic sacraments, and specific devotional prayer. These are support structures for many, but they do not corner the market on ways to pray as a community. Retreat settings allow for the exploration of other forms of communal prayer that can tap the creativity of planners and participants alike. Prayer of an informal nature—that would be inappropriate for the formal setting of Sunday worship—can be designed with the retreat in mind. Ritual and liturgical action that is specifically shaped by the readings and used during the retreat can be developed in a more personal and specific way. In addition to scriptural music, songs and recorded music that are meaningful can be used to highlight themes and dynamics within the retreat design.

In addition to eucharistic forms of communal worship, noneucharistic worship can also be incorporated. Increasingly within a church that has a shortage of ordained clergy, "paraliturgies," as these have sometimes been called, are becoming viable alternatives. The Word of God is used within these liturgies, along with music and reflection. And these paraliturgies can easily be led by nonordained persons. Communal experiences of prayer that utilize effective ritual or gesture, woven together with the traditional elements of worship, are sometimes powerful experiences of the Holy for people who have a limited exposure to worship. These experiences can be profoundly touching. Taking the time to develop symbolism and new scriptural interpretations can greatly enrich the private and communal life of retreatants.

Selecting the Type of Worship

In designing the worship portion of the retreat, the planners must, first of all, ascertain which type of worship suits the situation of the retreat the best. Would a eucharistic liturgy be helpful? Do the retreatants expect a eucharistic experience to complete their time of retreat? Is a noneucharistic prayer service of greater value? How is this apparent to the planners? Some practicalities have to be kept in mind when making these plans:

- What is the availability of an ordained priest for this retreat? This is essential when considering eucharistic liturgies. If this is a desirable aspect of the retreat and there is no ordained clergyperson among those attending, groups may need to consider joining with other retreat groups present at the retreat center for joint liturgies. This may shape the planning of the Eucharist out of consideration for the different foci of the retreat groups in attendance.
- What is the time-line for the entire event? Shorter events may have less time to devote exclusively to liturgical prayer and, therefore, it might be more appropriate to build it into a prayer service.
- What is the most suitable placement for communal worship within the entire schedule? If the closing of the retreat involves communal worship, the time frame may need to be extended to include closing remarks, thank you's, and final instructions.

Answers to some of these simple questions may shape the decision as to which type of liturgy to plan and how to implement it gracefully within the format of the retreat as a whole. The placement of the liturgies within the daily schedule may also put limits around the planners. If a eucharistic liturgy is limited by the scheduling of a meal following it, we as planners will need to respectfully frame our planning with this in mind. If a Mass is planned for early morning, sensitivity to the "early morning" rhythm of people will also have to be taken into account. If a liturgy involves sharing, ample time will have to be allotted so that it can be done without pressure.

Selecting Scripture and Readings

If the retreat team has already surfaced meaningful scriptural texts for the input sessions, liturgical planners can build on these images. To complement these or add to the scriptural references, readings for the liturgy can be selected from those of that particular day in the lectionary, or alternatives can be selected according to the focus of the retreat. Many retreat houses follow the liturgical cycle, using the readings of the day during the daily Mass. It is then the responsibility of the homilist to tie in the themes of the day to the themes of the retreat process. In small, private group experiences, it is justifiable for a retreat team to substitute scriptural readings into the Eucharist in order to illustrate their theme more thoroughly. Planners should consider both options in their initial meetings. "How can we best focus the retreatants and let the experience of worship deepen the messages that are being opened up for those attending?"— this is the question we as retreat planners must answer.

At times, nonscriptural readings hold great meaning for building themes within a retreat. Certainly, pieces of poetry and prose can be included in a prayer service and woven in to further illustrate the theme of the retreat. Often the method for reading or proclaiming creative pieces during prayer services can be done in unusual ways to further their impact. Choral reading in groups, individuals reading specific sections, and readings proclaimed from different parts of the room are but a few of the ways that readings can be done in a creative fashion.

Paraliturgical Format

While there are as many creative ways to pray as there are individuals, one format that has worked in the planning of noneucharistic paraliturgies is a simple form, incorporating music, readings, a meaningful action, and closing prayers. The format could resemble this:

- *Opening Prayer* and/or song
- Period of recollection: quieting or centering time
- *Reading*: done slowly with expression
- Response to the reading: a psalm or sung refrain
- *Reflection on the reading*: A homily or sharing
- Integrative time: quiet, digestive period
- *Action*: ritual gesture that is in response to the reading
- Prayer of petition: composed prior to the retreat or during
- *Closing prayer and hymn*

The main elements of this design are Opening, Reading, Reflection, Action, and Closing. The other elements are a response to these or further facilitate the reflective process begun before or after them. Each of these can be embellished in different ways depending on the time limits, the focus on the retreat, the creativity of the planners, and the appropriateness within the overall design.

Ritual Action

A final few words may be helpful on the incorporation of ritual action within worship on a retreat. Within Catholic Christianity, ritual action is a familiar reality. All of our sacraments involve ritual action, using symbolic elements and gestures, for example, forming the sign of the cross with oil on the hands, pouring water, breaking bread and sharing it, lighting candles and passing the flame, and placing ashes on the forehead. Within retreats, gesture becomes heightened in worship because greater care and time can be given to it. A symbol can be more fully explored and a gesture explained in a way that brings out new dimensions to its significance.

Designing a ritual action for worship on a retreat involves embodying in a particular way the ideas emphasized in the retreat. The use of simple elements like water, fire, oil, earth, and incense carries potency from within our religious tradition. Additional elements come from biblical references, for example, seeds, bread, vines, cups, clay, and so forth. These can be utilized in a ritual gesture of which each person can partake.

The actual touch and movement makes the imagery come to life and personalizes it for each participant. Many believers find that the most powerful sacramental moments in our tradition are those which they must come forward individually to touch or be touched. Ritual action proceeds on that premise and allows us to build in concrete gestures that do just that.

Selections From a Retreat Sampler

Ritual gesture as outlined above is one of the most significant elements within communal worship. It allows for an individual to tie his or her private spiritual life through action to a larger body. The following scriptural images are offered with a brief suggested gesture that could be integrated into the worship component of a retreat. Some of these may be best suited for a noneucharistic liturgy.

The Seed

Use sunflower seeds as a focus spot for a guided meditation on the inner life that is growing within each retreatant, hidden but real. Let each person hold a seed in their hand, feeling its texture and shape. (Julian of Norwich's meditation on a hazelnut could be read as a supplement to this meditation.) Allow people to imagine the whole of their being in the seed, fragile and yet beautiful, held by God tenderly.

The Feeding

Speak of how we each bring something—for example, an ability to listen, to counsel well, to care for another—which feeds another at the table of the Eucharist. Let each person select an herb, a vegetable, or another ingredient that represents what they bring to the feeding of human persons and the earth. At the end of worship, combine the ingredients for a shared meal, for example, a soup, stew, casserole, or something of the kind.

The Forgiving Parent

Give each person a palm-size piece of clay and allow them to fashion a hand from it. With their imaginations, ask the retreatants to enter into the mind of God who creates all living beings and loves each cell. From this vantage point, how does God regard the mistakes of our lives?

The Shriveled Hand

Ask retreatants to study the veins in their hands and feet. What needs to be strengthened in them that would allow them to reach out? Ask the retreatants to wash the hands of each other and offer a blessing as they do so.

The Net

Ask retreatants to write on pieces of paper the various "trappings" (a grudge they hold, the need for control, and so forth) that they carry around with them as a security blanket. Let them stuff the pieces of paper in a sack/net and carry them through the day. Before Eucharist, let them bring these "trappings" to God at the offertory.

The Salt of the Earth

Compose a ritual where salt is placed on the tongue and a blessing is offered upon the person after the text is read, reassuring the retreatant that they are salt for the world.

The Light of the World

Use a candle, a bushel basket, and some cloth to decorate. Build on the notion of being in hiding and being asked to come out. After each session, change the arrangement so that the candle eventually is glowing brightly on top of the basket.

The Storm at Sea

Put fans around the room on low. Do a guided meditation, inviting participants to get into a boat with their eyes shut and set off into deep water. As the storm rises, increase the fans and let them continue imagining themselves with Jesus. What does he say or do for them? Let them journal afterwards.

The Pearl of Great Price

Identify a symbol of buried treasure for the centerspot of the worship space. Accent it with light and cloth. Allow people to add the names of the pearls of great price (their passion for God, their love for their children, and so forth) they carry by writing it on a small rock and putting it on the altar.

Notes From the Author

These are but nine of many images that can be developed liturgically on a retreat. The beauty of a retreat setting is that it provides a retreat director time to embellish the meanings of the symbols through alternative forms of expression like art, word, music, and prayer. Art forms like dance, movement, mantras, or mime are more feasible in paraliturgical prayer settings than at Eucharist.

The other benefit is that people can personalize the symbols. They can take the images in and ask themselves how these personally touch them. They are in a slowed down rhythm that encourages them to journal and reflect. They can take the time to sort through the questions provided and bring those to worship.

Worship allows all of the imagery to ripple forth so that participants' understandings can be broadened by the sharing of others. Prayer in small groups, individual spiritual direction, and reconciliation or penance can greatly enrich the experience of the sacraments and Scripture for those present.

If time is provided for personal reflection on a series of questions, it may be advantageous to offer the sacrament of penance, or to provide spiritual counsel. Often these experiences bring up many insights that retreatants want to share. However, it is wise to note that there are limits to the depths these insights can be addressed during the retreat experience, since the brevity of a retreat may not provide sufficient time to plumb old hurts. Counseling or direction after the retreat may be a more suitable forum to process those.

Evaluation and Feedback

Evaluating a retreat has been continuously helpful in preventing me from becoming complacent and comfortable in what I may assume is the Spirit speaking. It keeps me and the retreat process honest and always new. Evaluating the process allows me to step back and to observe and re-examine the whole spiritual tapestry, adding pieces to the design as my heart and soul become more open to the divine intervention in my life and in the retreat experience.

—J. D., PSYCHOTHERAPIST AND RETREAT FACILITATOR

In planning and implementing a retreat, we often get so involved in the preparation that we overlook a very important final step: evaluation and feedback. It is the step through which we as a team can assess how we felt the retreat experience went and what troubleshooting could be done to make things smoother for the next event. It is also our opportunity to find out from the retreatants if this experience was effective and formative for them. This input can serve as a corrective agent for further formation events as well as affirm that which was spiritually enriching in the retreat experience just completed.

Evaluation and Feedback

There are two aspects of evaluation which can provide input for the future planning of similar events. First, evaluation from within the team of planners is essential since we worked on the project from beginning to end. We also know some of the behind-the-scenes realities that can become key information with regard to the effectiveness of the design. The second aspect is that of feedback from the retreatants about their experience. Were their needs met on some level? Did the planning team anticipate accurately and sensitively the spiritual hungers of those for whom they were planning?

Team Evaluations

Evaluation by the team begins before the retreat has even begun. Planners need to engage in ongoing self-reflective approaches that allow a "check and balance" in the planning process. This proactive approach to evaluation raises the team's awareness throughout the retreat experience from planning to implementation. As a group, we can continually revise and note our observations, including our intuitions about the effectiveness of the plan. These notes can be passed on to future planners. Facilitators also can benefit from some of this information when they plan their input. After the event, evaluation flows more readily from this awareness which has been cultivated over the entire planning process.

The evaluation we are speaking of here is not one born out of a critical mind-set. Criticism generally stymies people's creativity and vitality. This evaluation is born out of a self-reflective attentiveness to the Spirit. We need to cultivate a gentle reflective attitude among ourselves with regard to our planning process and our collaboration with one another in preparing the design and performing the designated tasks.

If we allow ourselves to drop down internally into an awareness of the presence of the Holy Spirit and relax within that presence without judgment or chastisement, we will find our reflections on our work to be far more gentle and life-giving. An evaluation that "takes on the mind of Christ" in its style will be supportive and constructive for all of us. The "bigger picture" from the heart of God tempers any analytical harshness that can creep into evaluations. This approach allows the Spirit to broaden our human perceptions to see the experience from a larger perspective.

Within the team's evaluative process, two phases of evaluation may be helpful. Phase One is what we may call "the organic phase," during which the group begins a reflection by brainstorming what our initial impressions are of the retreat. Phase Two is a deliberate return to the goals and objectives to ascertain their fulfillment and determine how to improve the design appropriately.

Phase One: The Organic Phase

This begins with a simple question:

- What worked?

This question allows for an organic reflection and reveling to begin. By starting off with the positive, we anchor the evaluative process in affirmation. Sometimes we spend a lot of energy dwelling on what did not work and miss out on how much good was done. This phase of evaluation allows for time to revel in the success of the retreat. It is a savoring by the team of the effective moments when something good happened. The Spirit may have moved and retreatants were graced in that. A team needs time to relish the triumphs of hard work and celebrate together. A facilitator may want to record these on pieces of newsprint so that the list is visible for the entire group.

Once a positive foundation is laid, the next simple query can be posed:

- What did not work?

With this question, the team shifts to reflect on the experience in order to improve the design. Brainstorming together as a group may be one of the more effective ways to begin this portion of the evaluation. The facilitator of the evaluation process can help the team articulate their ideas, noting what elements did not work from each individual's perspective. These ideas can be recorded on newsprint for the entire group to see. Following this brainstorming process, Phase Two begins.

Phase Two: The Structured Assessment

Begin with the goals and objectives:

- How did we fulfill the goals and objectives outlined for the retreat?

This is a more structured reflection process, utilizing the goals and objectives of the original design as the criteria. In naming the spiritual needs, the first strategy of the five we've outlined in this feature, the team identified what the focus of the retreat should be, based on the underlying concern of the retreatants. The first step in evaluation by the team then is to return to the goals which form the philosophical basis for the retreat. The team can use these statements as the basis for evaluating effectiveness. Did the retreat accomplish each of these goals? A systematic review of each of the goals articulated previously will allow the team to more thoroughly assess the work.

The team then asks a second key question:

• How can we improve the retreat?

The feedback from participants becomes significant at this point. Their experience may invite the team to consider alternative plans for future designs.

Feedback From Participants

While we as the planning team can generate some information among ourselves about our effectiveness, input from the participants provides another perspective. Information from the retreatants can be gleaned from written feedback sheets before they leave the site. Questionnaires can be made up in advance and circulated during the final gathering of the group. Four basic questions form the foundation for feedback:

• What was helpful during this retreat?
• Was anything not helpful? Please explain.
• Any suggestions for improving this retreat?
• Further comments?

These are basic questions that can easily be answered in a relatively short time. A more detailed approach to feedback can be developed, based on these four questions. A more specific tool can be developed incorporating the following points:

- Use *the goals and objectives* to ascertain the participants' view of their fulfillment.
- *The schedule* can be outlined with space provided after each pertinent event, for example, input, prayer services, social events, and so forth.
- List *five significant elements* within the retreat experience and ask retreatants to circle on a continuum how effective was each element in their experience.

We must be aware that the more detailed the evaluation is, the longer the time needed to complete it. Also we must note that evaluation must be done with sensitivity to maintaining the retreat ambiance and not detracting from it by excessive analysis. We should not disrupt the retreatants' process and their savoring the retreat with our agenda. Rather, we invite their feedback as gently as we seek it from within our team evaluation.

The planning team can send home with the retreatants a feedback sheet or mail one out after the retreat. The percentage of responses, however, drops significantly once retreatants are out the door and we may not get substantive numbers returned to us to aid our evaluation.

Selections From a Retreat Sampler

The following evaluation design may be suitable for adaptation within a retreat:

EVALUATION FOR A SPIRITUALITY RETREAT

Date of Retreat

Facilitator's Name

The following *eight elements* were included in the retreat. First, please circle the ones that were most helpful. Then, prioritize the circled items as to which was the most helpful (#1 being most helpful):

_____ Meditations
_____ Introductory storytelling evening
_____ Guided imagery exercises
_____ Sharing spiritual stories
_____ Opening icebreakers
_____ Input: six spiritual practices
_____ Journaling time
_____ Closing liturgy

Your further comments on each of these circled events would be greatly appreciated:

Accommodations: How would you describe your experience of each of the following?

• Food:
• Lodging:
• Hospitality:

Any recommendations for future retreats?

Any last words?

Notes From the Author

Evaluation is a key opportunity for retreat planners to assess their work. It is always more enjoyable to frame the evaluative process within a meal and a celebration. Indeed, after a job well done, celebration is most appropriate. The team will enjoy the chance to come together in a social way and rejoice in the project. When I work with retreat teams, I frequently invite all the planners to join in a night out for dinner and conversation. It's a time to visit, relax, and recall the triumphs together.

Whether or not the retreat design will ever be done again, feedback and evaluation is a significant part of the continuing education of your retreat team. Information and insight about the various elements of the retreat can validate the team's intuitions about their design. Elements that were effective can be transferred into other formation events for use beyond this individual retreat. The planners can utilize the experience of the retreat and apply the benefits of their reflection to other projects to which they will lend themselves.

Self-Care for the Retreat Director

I have a daily invitation. I am invited to choose life. I am invited to come to Jesus' table. Will my busyness keep me from daily being filled? Will all the noise of this world keep me from hearing the invitation, "Come to me." I cannot give what I have not first received. I come to you, Lord. Fill me.

—B. S., MARRIAGE ENCOUNTER RETREAT DIRECTOR

The experience of an effective retreat with receptive retreatants can provide great enjoyment and satisfaction for planners. But that satisfaction is no substitute for our personal spiritual practice of prayer, contemplation, and rejuvenation. Sustaining our own spiritual vitality through self-care is a concern for us because as leaders we model healthy integration of the messages ingrained within the retreat design. The strategies outlined in this text help us to nourish our own spiritual lives as we prepare for the blessed task of journeying with those in search of the living God. However, "the work" of a retreat director is still work. We must also nourish our own inner souls by discovering what keeps us fresh and focused.

What are some means that can aid us in our own balance? Six suggestions follow that may be applicable for our health while in retreat ministry.

1. *Leave ample time in the retreat schedule for re-creation for the facilitators and planners.* In designing a retreat, it is essential to build in rest spots for ourselves as facilitators. We all need breathing time. The retreatants need our time, but they also need their solitude. So do we who are behind the scenes. Some retreat designs are so congested with events that the planners leave the retreat exhausted. This exhaustion has repercussions in our home life and relationships beyond the walls of the retreat house. It can plant bad seeds among the family members and associates who must pick

up the pieces after the retreat or suffer the consequences of our tiredness.

The intensity of the retreat can also falsify the movements of the Holy Spirit in an experience of a temporary "high" near the end of the retreat, only to be followed by a crash and deflation in retreatants and directors alike after the retreat. Better to pace ourselves and allow the gentle Spirit some organic time to move people's hearts than to inflate the time with excessive stimulation.

As directors, we will be wise to pace our own time on retreat so that we do not burn out prematurely and impair our effectiveness in the long run. A more measured use of our time will protect us from becoming overwhelmed, cross, and disingenuous in our ministry.

2. *Don't schedule retreats too close together.* If retreat direction is a major component of our ministry, "overscheduling" can become death-dealing. We may shortchange the recuperative time we need for ourselves between formation processes. We can get into a functional way of being, going through the process without really entering into it ourselves. This can flatten our enthusiasm and dampen the delight for the work we do.

   Periodically, we may need to take "sabbatical periods" from the retreat ministry in order to restock our own interiors. This may be an essential practice of self-care for us. We are in an intense ministry, often dealing with very personal matters in other people's lives. We may be brought into trauma, abuse, fears, and scars from which it will be hard to recover. It will be crucial for our own well-being to recognize the signs inside ourselves of fatigue, frustration, and the thinning of our own relationship with God. Then, we can be proactive in thwarting a meltdown or saturation of our souls due to the intensity of the material we are dealing with and its effects on our own health.

3. *We must know our limits in the midst of the delicate demands of retreat ministry and set appropriate boundaries.* During retreats, the fragility of the human person is often brought into view. Retreat directors are privy to that primal disclosure. The very nature of retreat exposes the vulnerabilities and wounded parts of people. It can open them up for healing and forgiveness. To respond to this readiness and facilitate the healing, reconciliation has often been a part of retreat processes.

   We as directors need to be available in these crucial moments. They carry precious possibilities for the retreatants' revitalization. The circumstances may require extra time and energy from us. Yet, as we attend to these encounters, we must also be able to set some respectful boundaries around our time. We may need to call in help from other staff members so that we can focus and prepare internally for the next demand.

   Youth retreat directors may experience this more acutely than others. The very nature of adolescence requires extra attentiveness. Youth retreats can trigger a response from teenagers that opens them up to their own suffering, their God, and the yearning in their own hearts. Often, access to the spiritual and developmental issues of adolescents occurs in the late-night hours. The masks come down and the vulnerability is apparent.

   Youth retreat directors must have the resilience to be present during this, but also need to set boundaries that will allow time for sleep and rejuvenation. It is difficult when our energies flag to maintain an enthusiasm and attentiveness, especially when we are lacking in sleep and solitude. Recuperative time between retreats can help us undergo our own reconstruction and aid our reconnection with the Divine.

4. *We must be honest with ourselves about how we are connecting with or not connecting with God personally.* Self-deception is a phenomenal human tendency. Most of us have heard people in ministry proclaim—on occasion—that "my work is my prayer." While the nature of retreat work leads us into the most intimate areas of spirituality and human desire, it does not replace our need for the grooming of our own souls in relationship to God that prayer provides. If we have an established prayer rhythm in our everyday life, this will often be disrupted when we are giving a group retreat. That disruption does not erase the need for deliberate private prayer and meditation. Without this, our ministry as retreat directors will falter. Personal quiet time is as essential as sleep and recreation for the retreat director. We fool ourselves if we think we can get along without it.

   Our retreat ministry may require us to become more creative in how we realize the call to personal prayer. We may need to take a day away after the retreat to rest and restore our rhythm of prayer. We may need to do a "desert day" once a month instead of the traditional "holy hour" daily. We may need to tie in personal prayer to our evaluation process with our team, building in a time of solitude as we process the insights of the retreat. In whatever way serves us and serves God, we must honestly attend to our own inner wells. We cannot neglect our own need for intimacy for very long without discovering one day that our inner fire has diminished to an ember.

5. *Develop a support network of other spirituality professionals.* This system of support is absolutely necessary when we must limit our sharing because of confidentiality issues. We need other persons, who are dedicated to ministry, with whom we can share. These professionals should extend beyond our supervisors and personal spiritual directors. The network which we build can help us process our experience, provide

new ideas for development, and offer us safe haven for laughter, tears, and brainstorming.

6. *Sustain ongoing spiritual direction.* Every well runs dry. In the retreat ministry, it is easy to lose focus and perspective about our own spiritual state. Don't risk it. Take precautions. Spiritual directors can help us sort through our feelings and questions, bringing new insight and awareness to what we do and who we are. They are our personal lifelines. They can help us adjust to the curve balls that life throws us, so that we are less prone to getting caught off guard. Spiritual directors also help us discern our own tendency towards self-deception. We need them to reflect back to us the blemishes and beauty within ourselves so that we can offer all of that to God. Then, God can take our gifts and use them as God wills.

Our own self-care is vital in helping to sustain us in any ministry. In the ministry of retreats, we can find our reserves depleted through many late nights, acute needs, and spiritual struggles. It is essential that we take our own relationship with God seriously enough to minister to ourselves. In doing so, we model a care for the temple of God that is built into our very flesh.

Appendix

~

A Brief History of the Retreat Movement
in the United States

My Cursillo experience taught me the difference between
"good, old plastic Jesus" and seeing him as a living, breathing entity with whom I could have a personal relationship. After working in the Cursillo Movement I realized
that Christianity had little to do with a "church building"
and much more to do with building a community within
and outside the Church.

—A. C. D., FORMER CURSILLO COORDINATOR
AND MOTHER OF FIVE

The contemporary Retreat Movement is a part of a much larger
renewal dynamic that began as a grass-roots phenomenon
within the early years of the last century. Throughout the world,
Roman Catholicism was experiencing a movement of reform within
four areas of its ecclesial life. In the early 1900s, scriptural study within
the Roman Catholic Church took on a new energy. The Church
joined other biblical scholars and academicians in integrating into
their biblical research the insights gained from archeology, history,
and sociology. Ecumenical conversations in the area of Scripture
surged. Secondly, in the area of liturgy, grass-roots concern with the
renewal of the liturgical life of Roman Catholic worship was paving
the way for changes that would eventually be realized in the Second
Vatican Council. Finally, many papal encyclicals and documents were
pioneering in their call for social reform and social action, support-

ing the need for laborers to unionize and demand just wages and safe working conditions. Within the tumult of these renewal movements, spiritual renewal also reached its advent. Retreats for groups, individuals, and parishes were one form through which this call to renewal manifested itself.

Numerous forms of retreat emerged. Traditional forms that were already in existence included thirty-day and eight-day directed retreats for individuals following an Ignatian format. Preached retreats for groups and interest-group retreats, which had a specific focus based on the concerns of the group involved, developed. Most noteworthy in the United States and Canada were men's retreats, and later women's retreats. Out of each of these, a national movement emerged to promote spiritual renewal through the practice of retreat.

With the support of the Second Vatican Council, other retreat forms developed. The Encounter Movement spawned many forms such as Marriage Encounter and Engaged Encounter for the support of married couples. Similar to these, Cursillo and its reunion gatherings of Ultreya swept over the United States, having been imported from Spain. The Charismatic Renewal also brought spiritual refreshment for many who desired to more actively integrate the affective dimension of their persons into their spiritual life and prayer. Youth ministry retreats sprung up with the development of Teens Encounter Christ (TEC), Search, and sacramental preparation in the form of confirmation retreats.

A significant phenomenon in twentieth-century American Catholicism, therefore, has been the Retreat Movement among laity. While a comprehensive history has not yet been written, some significant dates have been compiled on the following page to illustrate this development.

Historical Chronology of the Lay Retreat Movement in the United States

The Lay Retreat Movement is almost a century old in the United States and Canada.

1909: Catholic men begin to gather for retreat.

1928: National Catholic Laymen's Retreat Conference is organized.

1934: National Laywomen's Retreat Movement promotes development of retreats for women.

The Retreat Movement's development was interrupted by World War II, but a resurgence occurred within the 1950s and 1960s with over half a million served annually on retreat.

1977: National Catholic Laymen's Retreat Conference merges with the National Catholic Laywomen's Retreat Movement and forms Retreats International.

In the 1960s, there were 400 retreat houses with 2000 full-time directors. Today, there are over 575 retreat centers in Retreats International alone with over one million served annually.

Bibliographical Resources for Planning Group Retreats, Days of Recollection, and Prayer Services

~

Planning

Be Still: Designing and Leading Contemplative Retreats, by Jane Vennard (Bethesda, MD: Alban Institute, 2000).

The Retreat Handbook, by Sandy and Larry Reimer (Wilton, CT: Morehouse-Barlow, 1986).

Group Retreats for Adults

Praying With Body and Soul: A Way to Intimacy With God, by Jane Vennard (Minneapolis, MN: Augsburg Fortress Publishers, 1998).

Retreat Resources: Retreats for Adults, Vol. 2, ed. Maury Smith, OFM (New York, NY: Paulist Press, 1976).

Young Adult Works, Binder #4, by Center for Ministry Development (Naugatuck, CT: Center for Ministry Development, 2000).

Group Retreats for Youth and Children

Retreats (Access Guide to Youth Ministries Series), by Reynolds Ekstrom (New Rochelle, NY: Don Bosco Multimedia, 1991).

Growing With Jesus: Retreats With Children, by Maryann Hakowski (Notre Dame, IN: Ave. Maria Press, 1993).

Teens Encounter Christ, by Andre Cirino, OFM, Francine Rogers (Canfield, OH: Alba Books, 1978).

Time With Jesus: Twenty Guided Meditations for Youth, by Thomas F. Catucci (Notre Dame, IN: Ave Maria, 1993).

Vine and Branches, Vols. 1–3, by Maryann Hakowski (Notre Dame, IN: Ave Maria Press, 1994).

Reconciliation

Celebrating Forgiveness: 15 Penance Celebrations, by Rev. William J. Koplik and Joan Brady (Mystic, CT: Twenty-Third Publications, 1985).

Parish Reconciliation Services: Seasonal Celebrations for Adults and Children, by Margrit A. Banta (Mystic, CT: Twenty-Third Publications, 1994).

Reconciliation Services for Children: 18 Prayer Services to Celebrate God's Forgiveness, by Gwen Costello (Mystic, CT: Twenty-Third Publications, 1992).

Prayer Services

Pentecost, Peanuts, Popcorn, Prayer: Prayer Services for High School Students, by Barbara Black, Karen Jessie, John M. Paulett (Villa Maria, PA: The Center for Learning, 1988).

Seasonal Prayer Services for Teenagers, by Greg Dues (Mystic, CT: Twenty-Third Publications, 1991).

Teen Prayer Services: 20 Themes for Reflection, by S. Kevin Regan (Mystic, CT: Twenty-Third Publications, 1992).

Twenty More Teen Prayer Services, by S. Kevin Regan (Mystic, CT: Twenty-Third Publications, 1994).

Supplementary Resources

Includes material for meditations, stories, prayer sessions, and personal growth for retreat directors.

The Art of Theological Reflection, by Patricia O'Connell Killen and John De Beer (New York, NY: Crossroad, 1994).

Liturgical Gestures, Word, Objects, from Center for Pastoral Liturgy, ed. Eleanor Bernstein, CSJ (Notre Dame, IN: Notre Dame University, 1995). [*A Retreat resource for creating meaningful liturgy, worship, and prayer in a retreat.*]

Meditations With Merton, by Nicki Verploegen Vandergrift (Liguori, MO: Liguori Publications, 1993).

Organic Spirituality: A Sixfold Path for Contemplative Living, by Nicki Verploegen Vandergrift (Maryknoll, NY: Orbis, 2000).

Orientations: A Collection of Helps for Prayer, Vol. 1, by John A. Veltri, SJ (Guelph, ONT: Loyola House, 1979).

Rites of Justice: The Sacraments and Liturgy as Ethical Imperatives, by Megan McKenna (Maryknoll, NY: Orbis, 1997).

Spirituality of Imperfection: Storytelling and the Journey to Wholeness, Ernest Kurtz and Katherine Ketcham (New York, NY: Bantam, 1993).

The Shattered Lantern: Rediscovering a Felt Presence of God, by Ronald Rolheiser (New York, NY: Crossroad, 2001).

The Third Spiritual Alphabet, by Francisco de Osuna (New York, NY: Paulist, 1981).